DIANA ROSS

DIANA ROSS

John Wyeth, Jr.

CHELSEA HOUSE PUBLISHERS
Philadelphia

Chelsea House Publishers

Editorial Director   Richard Rennert
Executive Managing Editor   Karyn Gullen Browne
Copy Chief   Robin James
Picture Editor   Adrian G. Allen
Creative Director   Robert Mitchell
Art Director   Joan Ferrigno
Production Manager   Sallye Scott

Black Americans of Achievement

Senior Editor   Philip Koslow

Staff for DIANA ROSS

Editorial Assistant   Scott D. Briggs
Senior Designer   Marjorie Zaum
Picture Researcher   Villette Harris
Cover Illustrator   Bradford Brown

The Chelsea House World Wide Web address is
http://www.chelseahouse.com

  5 7 9 8 6

Library of Congress Cataloging-in-Publication Data
Wyeth, John, Jr.
Diana Ross : entertainer / John Wyeth, Jr.
    p. cm. — (Black Americans of achievement)
  Includes bibliographical references and index.
Summary: Describes a benefit concert in Central Park starring this
Afro-American entertainer and then relates her career as a singer.
   ISBN   0-7910-1882-2.
               0-7910-1911-X (pbk.)
   1. Ross, Diana, 1944– —Juvenile literature.
2. Singers—United States—Biography—Juvenile literature. [1. Ross, Diana,
1944– 2. Singers. 3. Afro-Americans—Biography. 4. Women—Biography.]
I. Title.
ML3930.R67W94 1996   95-23332
782.42'1644'092—dc20   CIP
[B]   ACMN

Frontispiece: *Diana Ross,
photographed at a New York
City restaurant on January
12, 1973, when she received
the* Cue *magazine Entertainer
of the Year Award.*

CONTENTS

BLACK AMERICANS OF ACHIEVEMENT

HENRY AARON
baseball great

KAREEM ABDUL-JABBAR
basketball great

MUHAMMAD ALI
heavyweight champion

MAYA ANGELOU
author

LOUIS ARMSTRONG
musician

JOSEPHINE BAKER
entertainer

TYRA BANKS
model

BENJAMIN BANNEKER
scientist and mathematician

COUNT BASIE
bandleader and composer

ANGELA BASSETT
actress

ROMARE BEARDEN
artist

HALLE BERRY
actress

MARY MCLEOD BETHUNE
educator

GEORGE WASHINGTON CARVER
botanist

JOHNNIE COCHRAN
lawyer

BILL COSBY
entertainer

MILES DAVIS
musician

FREDERICK DOUGLASS
abolitionist editor

CHARLES DREW
physician

PAUL LAURENCE DUNBAR
poet

DUKE ELLINGTON
bandleader and composer

RALPH ELLISON
author

JULIUS ERVING
basketball great

JAMES FARMER
civil-rights leader

LOUIS FARRAKHAN
political activist

ELLA FITZGERALD
singer

ARETHA FRANKLIN
entertainer

MORGAN FREEMAN
actor

MARCUS GARVEY
black nationalist leader

WHOOPI GOLDBERG
entertainer

DANNY GLOVER
actor

CUBA GOODING JR.
actor

ALEX HALEY
author

PRINCE HALL
social reformer

JIMI HENDRIX
musician

MATTHEW HENSON
explorer

GREGORY HINES
performer

BILLIE HOLIDAY
singer

LENA HORNE
entertainer

WHITNEY HOUSTON
singer and actress

LANGSTON HUGHES
poet

JANET JACKSON
musician

JESSE JACKSON
civil-rights leader and politician

MICHAEL JACKSON
entertainer

SAMUEL L. JACKSON
actor

T. D. JAKES
religious leader

MAE JEMISON
astronaut

MAGIC JOHNSON
basketball great

SCOTT JOPLIN *composer*	TERRY MCMILLAN *author*	JACKIE ROBINSON *baseball great*	MADAM C. J. WALKER *entrepreneur*
BARBARA JORDAN *politician*	RONALD MCNAIR *astronaut*	CHRIS ROCK *comedian and actor*	BOOKER T. WASHINGTON *educator*
MICHAEL JORDAN *basketball great*	TONI MORRISON *author*	DIANA ROSS *entertainer*	DENZEL WASHINGTON *actor*
CORETTA SCOTT KING *civil-rights leader*	ELIJAH MUHAMMAD *religious leader*	AL SHARPTON *minister and activist*	J. C. WATTS *politician*
MARTIN LUTHER KING, JR. *civil-rights leader*	EDDIE MURPHY *entertainer*	WILL SMITH *actor*	VANESSA WILLIAMS *singer and actress*
QUEEN LATIFAH *singer/actress*	JESSE OWENS *champion athlete*	WESLEY SNIPES *actor*	VENUS WILLIAMS *tennis star*
LEWIS LATIMER *scientist*	SATCHEL PAIGE *baseball great*	CLARENCE THOMAS *Supreme Court justice*	OPRAH WINFREY *entertainer*
SPIKE LEE *filmmaker*	CHARLIE PARKER *musician*	SOJOURNER TRUTH *antislavery activist*	TIGER WOODS *golf star*
CARL LEWIS *champion athlete*	ROSA PARKS *civil-rights leader*	HARRIET TUBMAN *antislavery activist*	
MALCOLM X *militant black leader*	COLIN POWELL *military leader*	NAT TURNER *slave revolt leader*	
BOB MARLEY *musician*	DELLA REESE *entertainer*	TINA TURNER *entertainer*	
THURGOOD MARSHALL *Supreme Court justice*	PAUL ROBESON *singer and actor*	ALICE WALKER *author*	

ON
ACHIEVEMENT

⚫

Coretta Scott King

Before you begin this book, I hope you will ask yourself what the word *excellence* means to you. I think that it's a question we should all ask, and keep asking as we grow older and change. Because the truest answer to it should never change. When you think of excellence, perhaps you think of success at work; or of becoming wealthy; or meeting the right person, getting married, and having a good family life.

Those important goals are worth striving for, but there is a better way to look at excellence. As Martin Luther King, Jr., said in one of his last sermons, "I want you to be first in love. I want you to be first in moral excellence. I want you to be first in generosity. If you want to be important, wonderful. If you want to be great, wonderful. But recognize that he who is greatest among you shall be your servant."

My husband, Martin Luther King, Jr., knew that the true meaning of achievement is service. When I met him, in 1952, he was already ordained as a Baptist preacher and was working toward a doctoral degree at Boston University. I was studying at the New England Conservatory and dreamed of accomplishments in music. We married a year later, and after I graduated the following year we moved to Montgomery, Alabama. We didn't know it then, but our notions of achievement were about to undergo a dramatic change.

You may have read or heard about what happened next. What began with the boycott of a local bus line grew into a national movement, and by the time he was assassinated in 1968 my husband had fashioned a black movement powerful enough to shatter forever the practice of racial segregation. What you may not have read about is where he got his method for resisting injustice without compromising his religious beliefs.

He adopted the strategy of nonviolence from a man of a different race, who lived in a different country, and even practiced a different religion. The man was Mahatma Gandhi, the great leader of India, who devoted his life to serving humanity in the spirit of love and nonviolence. It was in these principles that Martin discovered his method for social reform. More than anything else, those two principles were the key to his achievements.

This book is about black Americans who served society through the excellence of their achievements. It forms a part of the rich history of black men and women in America—a history of stunning accomplishments in every field of human endeavor, from literature and art to science, industry, education, diplomacy, athletics, juris-prudence, even polar exploration.

Not all of the people in this history had the same ideals, but I think you will find something that all of them had in common. Like Martin Luther King, Jr., they all decided to become "drum majors" and serve humanity. In that principle—whether it was expressed in books, in-ventions, or song—they found something outside themselves to use as a goal and a guide. Something that showed them a way to serve others, instead of only living for themselves.

Reading the stories of these courageous men and women not only helps us discover the principles that we will use to guide our own lives but also teaches us about our black heritage and about America itself. It is crucial for us to know the heroes and heroines of our history and to realize that the price we paid in our struggle for equality in America was dear. But we must also understand that we have gotten as far as we have partly because America's democratic system and ideals made it possible.

We are still struggling with racism and prejudice. But the great men and women in this series are a tribute to the spirit of our democratic ideals and the system in which they have flourished. And that makes their stories special and worth knowing. ☙

1

RAIN WOMAN

❧

I T WAS THURSDAY, July 21, 1983, a hot, humid day even by midsummer New York standards. By 11:00 A.M., temperatures had soared into the nineties. But the sweltering heat was undaunting to the 4,000 fans who had already begun to congregate on the Great Lawn in New York City's Central Park in anticipation of the night's performance. Some had come with picnic lunches—one family had even brought a white tablecloth, champagne, and a gourmet luncheon. Others simply drank sodas and claimed their places as close to the stage as they could get. By late afternoon, the crowd had swelled to well over 100,000.

They had all come to see the legendary Diana Ross, who was scheduled to give a free concert that evening at six o'clock. Ross had agreed to hold the concert, paid for largely out of her own pocket, in order to raise money for the renovation of a playground in another part of Central Park. Sales of T-shirts, posters, and other souvenirs would help pay the cost of restoring the park. "It's for the children," said Ross of the project. "It's my dream."

When she published her memoir, *Secrets of a Sparrow*, Ross detailed her vision for the playground. She wrote that she wanted to create "a secure place where children could play, run, laugh, and meet other children, a place to be safe in the magical time of

Diana Ross performs before 400,000 fans in New York's Central Park on July 21, 1983. Ross organized the free concert in order to raise money for a playground in the park.

childhood, a wooden playground where little fingers would not get pinched."

The concert had been a huge undertaking involving months of planning, both for Ross and for the city of New York. One hundred forty amplifiers were positioned to carry Ross's voice to the huge audience, and two massive video screens, each over 20 feet high, were suspended four stories above the stage for the benefit of those fans who were too far away to actually see Ross perform. The concert was also slated to be broadcast on television around the world.

By the time six o'clock rolled around, between 350,000 and 400,000 people had packed into the 13-acre expanse of the Great Lawn. Even for Diana Ross, who had performed countless times in front of huge audiences—first as a member of the Supremes and then in her subsequent solo career—this was an event to be remembered. In recent years, free concerts in Central Park have become a summer tradition, but in the early 1980s only Elton John and Simon and Garfunkel had been willing to make the effort. Nelson George, an editor at *Billboard* magazine, complimented Ross on her decision to give a free concert for people who could not otherwise afford to see her. "With the Atlantic City prices she's getting," George wrote, "most black folks have never seen her perform live."

Shortly after 6:00 P.M., Ross hit the stage amid a troupe of dancers in traditional African garb. She wore a multicolored straw veil but shortly threw it aside to reveal a sparkling orange bodysuit. The cheers of the audience swelled into powerful, seemingly endless waves. Finally, Ross launched into her opening number, the inspirational "Ain't No Mountain High Enough," one of the first singles she had released after leaving the Supremes in 1970 to pursue her solo career. "Ain't no mountain high enough,"

she sang. "Nothing in this world can keep me from you." The crowd went wild.

Ross continued her performance with "Stop! in the Name of Love," "Baby Love," and other songs that had launched her career with the Supremes almost 20 years earlier. But as she sang, rain began to patter on the lawn and the stage. Undaunted, Ross continued her performance. "I've waited a lifetime to get here," she shouted triumphantly to the crowd, "and I'm not going anywhere."

The audience was certainly not about to walk out on the spectacular show. They stood their ground as the wind picked up and the rain came down more heavily. Some fans danced joyously while others simply stared at the stage transfixed. New York's mayor, Edward Koch, watched from underneath his umbrella, his well-shined shoes sinking into the deepening mud of the Great Lawn. Ross's orange cape, which had been thrown over her shoulders when the clouds first opened, fluttered gently and then began to blow wildly in the wind. Several times the concert staff and the park officials tried to coax

An aerial view of Central Park, looking south, shows the immense crowd gathered on the Great Lawn at the start of Ross's July 21 concert. Unfortunately, a powerful thunderstorm erupted 45 minutes into the show, causing Ross to reschedule her performance for the following evening.

her off the stage, but she continued to sing with her makeup dripping down her face in great black streaks. "I opened my arms wide," she later wrote. "I moved them back and forth, arresting any personal resistance that had surfaced. I merged with the pouring water. I let it in. I became a part of it, it became a part of me. Rain and woman were one. Now I was a rain woman."

When the shower became a torrential downpour, even Ross had to admit that it was time to stop the music. Nevertheless, she remained on the stage for some time, urging the crowd to disperse in an orderly fashion so that no one would get hurt. Anyone who has ever been to a rock concert or sporting event knows that large crowds can sometimes get unruly— in the midst of crashing thunder and lightning, the chance of a dangerous panic was even greater. Ross was determined to prevent this. "This was my dream," she recalled. "I was the captain, and I would not abandon ship. . . . I took charge. I would be the last to leave after I was certain that everyone else was safe."

New York's commissioner of parks and recreation, Henry J. Stern, was quoted the following day in the *New York Times* as saying that Ross "was magnificent in calming the crowd and gradually emptying the Great Lawn." Amazingly, there were very few injuries or problems that night. Many of the concertgoers turned the deluge into a chance to have some fun, engaging in mud fights as they slogged their way out of the park.

Finally satisfied that her fans were leaving the park safely, Ross left the stage and returned to her nearby apartment. She quickly phoned her children, who had been whisked away from the concert to Ross's Connecticut home by concerned staff members. After assuring herself that the children were all right, Ross watched with some disappointment the

Determined to gratify her fans, Ross belts out a song at her second Central Park concert on July 22. This time the rain held off, and 300,000 New Yorkers thrilled to Ross's artistry.

news broadcasts about her rained-out performance and then went to sleep.

When Ross saw the next day's newspapers she discovered that her show had gone over well with the critics, despite its untimely end. One reviewer, Kenny Solms, called Ross's performance "electric." "She almost stopped the rain," Solms wrote. "Now there are five elements: earth, wind, fire, ice . . . and Diana."

Still, Ross was not satisfied. She could not allow herself to be deflected from her goal, even by powerful forces of nature. And so, without wasting time lamenting over the previous night, she and her staff planned a repeat performance to be held that evening.

The weather was perfect on July 22, (with the exception of the continuing heat wave, which true fans took in stride), and Act Two went on as scheduled. As expected, the crowd was a bit smaller—many of those who had attended the previous night were afraid of being caught in another storm. But the concert possessed the same energy, and the audience was lavishly rewarded.

This time, Ross focused less on her older numbers and more on her recent material. There was a breathless, almost religious feel to the performance—at one point Ross read excerpts from Khalil Gibran's book *The Prophet*—that was much different from the catchy pop classics of the Supremes era. Those who attended the second concert saw another side of Diana Ross. She performed "Home," a hit from her 1978 movie, *The Wiz*; "Ribbon in the Sky," a song that Stevie Wonder had written for her; and the duet "Endless Love" with an anonymous male singer who crouched below her in the orchestra pit.

As the concert drew to a close several hours later, Ross called out to the audience for requests. "I don't have to disappear. I don't want to leave. You're

Accompanied by Mayor Ed Koch (center) and Parks Commissioner Henry Stern, Ross takes part in the groundbreaking ceremony for her playground. After anticipated revenues from the Central Park concerts failed to materialize, Ross paid the $275,000 construction costs out of her own pocket.

wonderful. I love you. Bless you all. You've been so good to me." She performed her final encore, and the fans began to disperse.

This time, however, the exodus from the park was neither peaceful nor playful. Perhaps as a result of the suffocating heat that blanketed the park, bands of youths began to run amok, attacking and robbing anyone they came across. In one unpleasant incident, 15 youths invaded the patio of Central Park's posh restaurant, Tavern on the Green, tipping over tables and assaulting patrons. Police reinforcements swept into the park, and for the most part the ruckus ended by 11:00 P.M. Unfortunately, the outbreak of violence fixed the event in the minds of New Yorkers as much as Ross's performances. One local radio station, WNEW, referred to the hours following the Friday concert as "the night New York was mugged."

Despite the unfortunate incidents following the show, no one ever faulted Ross for the violence. She tried, not once but twice, to hold a show that would raise money to rebuild a children's playground, a worthy cause by any standard. And although the shows were ultimately a financial disaster for everyone involved, Ross donated her own money for the playground, which opened in September 1986 at the corner of 81st Street and Central Park West. The children who now ride on the seesaws or climb on the jungle gym may not know who made the dream a reality, but that was never an issue for Ross. "There are few people who know," she later wrote, "but that's not important. What does matter is that as you read this, children are having fun and running and laughing and safely playing with each other. And their parents can know that while they are there, in the playground of my dreams, they are safe and secure. Come rain or shine." ❧

2

"I'M GOING TO BE A SINGER"

‹‹❀››

When Diane Ross graduated from Detroit's prestigious Cass Technical High School in 1962, her classmates voted her the best-dressed girl. At this time, the stylish and talented teenager was already on her way to a successful singing career.

DIANA ROSS WAS born on March 26, 1944, in Detroit, Michigan. One of the world's great inland ports, Detroit had been the center of the nation's automobile industry since the 1910s, its skyline dominated by industrial architecture such as Ford's giant River Rouge plant on the banks of the Detroit River. During the 1930s, Detroit had been hit hard by the Great Depression. But during the 1940s, when the United States was embroiled in World War II and the great auto plants began to churn out planes and tanks for the armed forces, Detroit began to boom again, attracting workers from all parts of the country. Many black families in particular, frustrated with the poverty and racial discrimination rampant in the South, found new hope and opportunity in the bustling factories of Detroit and other northern industrial cities.

Fred Ross, Diana's father, had come to Detroit from Bluefield, West Virginia, to live with his aunt in 1926, when he was six years old. Always a hard worker, he spent his after-school hours working in the laundry business his aunt owned and operated. Despite the hours he devoted to work, Ross was able to graduate from Detroit's highly selective Cass Technical High School in 1937, and he went on to study business administration at Wayne State College while also working full time for the U.S. Postal Service.

Ross was soon approached by a firm named Briggs Manufacturing, which offered him a better-paying job if he agreed to box on the company-sponsored team. (Ross had won a number of boxing competitions at Wayne State, and at one point he advanced as far as the semifinals in a Golden Gloves middleweight competition.) At this time, Ross met Ernestine Moten at a friend's house, and the two struck up a close friendship that led eventually to marriage.

A native of Allenville, Alabama, Moten was the daughter of a Baptist minister. She had grown up in a strict household where religion played a dominant role. Moten was an accomplished singer who had won a number of vocal competitions as a child, but she considered a career in music a frivolous venture and chose instead to enter Selma University in Alabama. After attending college, she decided to move to Detroit, where her sister was already living.

In Detroit, Moten occasionally sang in talent contests at such clubs as the Three Sixes, the El Casino, and the Club Chorus Girl. She was popular with the crowds at these venues, but she was still reluctant to consider a career in music.

Ross and Moten were married in March 1941 after Ross had finished his studies at Wayne State. The couple's first child, Barbara Jean, was born in June 1942, and Diana followed two years later.

In fact, the name Diana Ross, which later became known to millions of people around the world, was due in part to a clerical error. Ernestine Ross intended to name her second child Diane, and her family and close friends have always called her by this name. However, the name appeared on the birth certificate as Diana; as her musical career developed, Ross finally

decided to use the name bestowed on her by the hospital worker who filled out her birth certificate.

Three months after Diane was born, Fred Ross was drafted into the U.S. Army, where he served for two years. Ernestine Ross, a hard worker just like her husband, supported her family in the interim by teaching adult sewing classes and later teaching kindergarten. Fred traveled the world during World War II, spending time in England, France, Belgium, and the South Pacific. Finally, as the war drew to its conclusion in 1945, he was able to return to his family in Detroit. At this point, Diane really got to know her father for the first time. "I was a baby when he left," she later wrote, "so he was a stranger to me by the time he was discharged."

By 1950, Fred and Ernestine Ross had three more children—Margretia, Fred junior, and Arthur, who was known as T-Boy (for "tiny boy," because of his small stature). For some time, the Ross family was able to maintain a relatively stable middle-class life-

A view of downtown Detroit during the early 1950s. The imposing, squarish building in the left-center portion of the photo housed J. L. Hudson's, the legendary department store where Diane Ross worked during her high school years.

style, although Fred senior was often forced to work two and even three jobs to support his growing brood. Despite the many demands on their budget, the Rosses always kept their children clean and well-dressed, and they were stern in their emphasis on education. This work ethic had a lasting effect on the children—from an early age, Diane was determined to succeed, although her parents would not always be pleased with the path she chose to take.

At the age of five, Diane entered Balch Elementary School, one of the best schools in the city. There she soon became known as a leader among the other children. In particular, her teachers remember the many dramatic productions she organized with her friends. As Diane's first-grade teacher recalled, "She had an uncanny ability to organize. . . . She knew what she wanted to do, so she set about doing it. She was not overbearing. What always impressed me about Diane was that she wanted to include her friends in any of the little programs that she organized. She was a sharing type of girl." Still, as the same teacher pointed out with a laugh, the star of these productions was always "Diane, who else?"

The same determination and fiery spirit also got Diane into a number of fights. Instructed by the generally mild Ernestine Ross never to back down to a bully, Diane took the advice to heart, defending both herself and her siblings in times of trouble. A school friend remembers, "Even though she was really skinny, she could take care of herself. She didn't like being pushed around and she wasn't afraid to do something about it." Often more interested in playing outdoors than participating in the traditional activities of a young girl, Diane became known as something of a tomboy. "I was a real close friend to all the bullies," she recalled in *Secrets of a Sparrow*. "I didn't really want anything then. I just wanted to have fun.

We used to kill chickens in garbage cans and we'd kill rats with bows and arrows."

But whatever trouble she may have gotten into as a youngster, Diane never forgot the quality education she received at Balch. Teachers remember that she came back to visit as she went on through junior high and high school. And in 1982, she donated a substantial sum of money to Balch so that other children could continue to benefit from the fine schooling she had received 30 years earlier.

In 1950, when Diane was six years old, her mother was stricken with a serious case of tuberculosis. Forced to reside in a hospital in Holland, Michigan, Ernestine could not care for her family, and Fred Ross found himself overwhelmed by the harsh reality of working long hours and caring for five children alone. Finally, Fred piled the children into a station wagon

In 1958, the Ross family moved into the Brewster-Douglass Projects, pictured here. At the time, the projects were well maintained, and they provided safe, affordable housing for Detroit's working-class citizens.

and drove them 750 miles to Bessemer, Alabama, to live with their aunt until Ernestine recovered. There, the Ross children spent much of their time with their grandparents, who had raised 12 children of their own.

In Alabama, Diane had her first taste of southern racism. She was required to drink from different fountains than white people, to eat in separate sections of restaurants, and to ride in the back of public buses—injustices that would soon become the target of the growing civil rights movement. But for nine-year-old Diane, who rarely encountered white people in the area of Alabama where she stayed, the experience was not especially painful. Only much later, on tour as a member of the Supremes, would she react strongly against the bigotry and violence that afflicted the region.

The most important feature of Diane's stay was her introduction to gospel music. Her grandfather was pastor at the Alabama Bessemer Baptist Church, and the children were constantly exposed to the rousing grandeur of the African-American musical tradition. In Bessemer, Diane's love for music was solidified.

After spending a year in the hospital, Ernestine Ross recovered and returned home, and the children moved back to Detroit. Here, Diane was newly aware of her musical surroundings, which included gospel and a great deal more. The new, vital sounds of rock and roll had begun to make inroads across the nation, and young Diane became fascinated with the rebellious music that crackled across the airwaves on transistor radios all over Detroit.

At this time she began to compete with her older sister, Barbara, a serious student who spent most of her time reading and studying. Barbara excelled at academics (she eventually went on to become a doctor), but Diane never lagged far behind. She continued to earn excellent grades while pursuing a wealth of outside interests—including singing.

Diane sang in the choir at Detroit's Olivet Baptist Church, a duty that had become something of a Ross family tradition. When her parents had visitors, Diane would often give impromptu performances. On one such occasion, Fred Ross decided to pass around a hat for his talented daughter, and he collected enough money to buy Diane the pair of patent leather shoes that she had been yearning for. He did not make a habit out of this, though, because he was too proud to beg, even on behalf of his children.

Shortly before Ernestine Ross had a sixth child (Wilbert Alex, known as Chico) in December 1955, the family moved to a larger house in Detroit's prosperous North End. Although Diane did not enjoy the two years she spent at her new school, Dwyer Junior High, she later had fond memories of the time she spent at the Rosses' beautiful new house. About this time, the first wave of soul music was beginning to hit the streets. One of the Rosses' neighbors was the singer Smokey Robinson, who would later achieve great fame along with his group the Miracles. (Diane knew Robinson's younger sister and tried to spend as much time at her friend's house as possible, in the hope of seeing her friend's increasingly famous brother.) The Miracles were the first vocal group signed by a fledgling soul label called Tamla, which would become an essential part of Diane's life for many years to follow.

Detroit's economy declined during the late 1950s as more and more workers competed for fewer jobs, and even the ambitious Fred Ross was forced to tighten his family's purse strings. On Diane's 14th birthday in 1958, the eight members of the Ross family moved to a new low-income housing development, the Brewster-Douglass Projects.

*Smokey Robinson (left),
pictured here with his group,
the Miracles, was a neighbor
of the Rosses while Diane
was growing up. Robinson's
growing success as a singer
fueled Diane's hopes of a
successful performing career.*

At the time, large housing projects were relatively new in American cities. Fred Ross later recalled that "a bad stigma hadn't yet been attached to the projects. The front yards had nice lawns, the houses were fairly decent. . . . In fact, it looked as nice as some of the buildings I see now that are being sold as condominiums!" Indeed, during the 1950s, the Brewster-Douglass Projects were a bustling, lively community of working-class people. It was here that the Supremes would eventually be born.

Like her father and her sister Barbara, Diane attended Cass Tech, the most prestigious high school in Detroit, where a B plus average was required for admission. Cass Tech drew the best students from all over Detroit. Although Diane had to deal with the "smart kid" stigma that plagued the children from her neighborhood who attended Cass, she was quite popular as a teenager.

Except for one grumpy drama teacher who dismissed her "weak voice," most of the faculty at Cass agreed that Diane was a gifted singer. Indeed, she found that she had a flair for many of the activities she pursued. She also excelled in Cass's clothing design courses and did well on the swimming team. Diane even found time for beauty school classes in the evenings, modeling classes on weekends, and a part-time job at Detroit's classiest department store, J. L. Hudson's. At Hudson's, Diane waited tables in one of the store's restaurants. She was said to have been one of the first black employees there who was allowed outside of the kitchen.

During her high school years, Diane began to feel that her interest in singing was not just a passing fancy. Although she maintained the necessary grades to remain at Cass, her teachers sometimes found that her mind was occupied by visions of fame and fortune. One teacher recalled asking Diane why she was daydreaming during a study hall instead of working: "[Diane] shot back, 'You know I'm going to be a singer, don't you?' and then she handed me a picture of the Temptations that she had carefully cut out of the *Detroit News*. She said, 'I sing on weekends.' Well, I looked at her and said to myself, 'Oh, you poor child! You'll never make it!' "

In January 1962, Diane graduated from Cass Tech and was voted the best-dressed girl in her class—quite an honor for a teenager who designed most of her own clothes. By this time, she was already on her way to stardom. ☙

3

HITSVILLE USA
·❦·

WITH THE FOURTH-LARGEST black population in the nation by the late 1950s, Detroit was becoming a thriving center of black music. Rhythm and blues was on the rise, paralleling the success of rock and roll in the "white world." For the most part, black audiences still listened to black performers. Chuck Berry, Little Richard, and the Drifters were all very popular with young African Americans.

Vocal groups, usually ranging from trios to quintets, dominated rhythm and blues at the time. In the Brewster-Douglass Projects, teenagers listened to this new music on stoops and corners and held informal vocal competitions in courtyards. Diane, often forbidden from staying out after dark by her strict parents, watched these exciting goings-on from her window, wanting badly to be a part of it all.

In this thriving atmosphere of African-American spontaneity and creativity, Berry Gordy, Jr., saw his window of opportunity. The son of a successful business entrepreneur, Gordy grew up with a strong work ethic but had no taste for the "nine-to-five" lifestyle of his father and grandfather before him. He dropped out of high school and tried to pursue a career in boxing. Although he was talented and quick on his feet, he realized that he did not have the potential to become a champion.

The legendary Chuck Berry performs his patented duckwalk at a 1965 concert. While Diane Ross was growing up, Berry and other great black artists, such as Little Richard and Sam Cooke, were gaining a nationwide audience for the dynamic sound of rhythm and blues.

After a stint in the U.S. Army, Gordy returned to Detroit in 1953 and opened a jazz record store with a loan from his father. During the two years that the store struggled to stay in business, he began to realize that jazz was losing its audience. More and more people wanted to hear the new sounds, rock and roll and rhythm and blues.

When his business went bankrupt, Gordy went to work on the assembly line at Ford Motors. He spent most of his free time writing songs and hanging out at jazz clubs like the Flame Show Bar, where two of his sisters worked at concession stands and introduced him to the musicians that frequented the bar. Gordy carried a suitcase filled with songs he had written and pursued the musicians relentlessly, trying to get someone to record one of his numbers. After several years of discouragement, Gordy met Jackie Wilson, who recorded a number of his songs, some with considerable success. One of them, "Reet Petite," reached number 11 on the rhythm and blues charts in 1957 and sold more than 250,000 copies.

After writing and producing a group of fairly popular songs, including Janie Bradford's hit single "Money (That's What I Want)," Gordy decided it was time to start his own record company. He was already working closely with Smokey Robinson and the Miracles, and Robinson reportedly encouraged him to make his move. Once again, Gordy asked for a family loan and stepped back into the uncertain world of music by forming Tamla Records.

Gordy's infectious enthusiasm soon had his whole family involved in helping to get Tamla Records off the ground. His ear for an appealing tune was unmatched, and his criterion for releasing a song was simple and direct—some of the company's early employees remember that Gordy would play them a song and ask them, "Would you buy this record for a dollar, or would you buy a sandwich?" Before long, many people were forsaking their sandwiches, opting instead for Tamla's popular singles.

Gordy recalled his inspiration for songwriting in the following terms: "Everybody was writing love songs. I was basically a dreamer of love songs, and that's what I wanted to write, too. But wanting to write love songs and also living in the real world and listening to the earthy problems of life, I tried to mix that up with the love and the feeling." At Tamla, this became a formula for successful songwriting. These songs told stories about life, straying from the lyrical gibberish that had been popular in rock and roll of the late 1950s and early 1960s—Little Richard's 1955 hit "Tutti Frutti" is a prime example.

Asked by an interviewer to describe the Motown sound (Tamla was renamed Motown in 1962), Gordy said, "We thought of the neighborhoods we were raised in, and came up with a six-word definition: Rats, roaches, struggle, talent, guts, love." Motown songs dealt with the gritty realities of life, but they always had a danceable beat. In 1959, Tamla had its first major hit with the Miracles' "Shop Around," which went to number one on the rhythm and blues charts and number two on the pop charts, selling more than 1 million copies.

With good fortune coming relatively fast, the offices of Tamla Records at 2648 West Grand Boulevard in Detroit (soon renamed Hitsville USA) became the central hangout for aspiring black singers, songwriters, and music groupies. Diane Ross was among the young people crowding the lobby of the plain, unassuming white house where the Tamla success story was unfolding. All the young dreamers hoped to meet the man himself, Berry Gordy, Jr., who would lead them to their own pot of gold.

Hitsville in the early 1960s was more than just a record factory. Ross remembered it as "a family experience, and it gave us things that our real families

Berry Gordy, Jr., (right) founded Tamla Records in 1958 and produced his first hit record the following year. By 1968, when he received this award from radio personality Barry Gray, he had built his small company into the multimillion-dollar entertainment giant known as Motown.

couldn't." For her, the extra ingredient was the encouragement—and the financial backing—she needed to become a successful entertainer. To emphasize the family atmosphere, Gordy often provided home-cooked meals for the people who clustered around Motown; and many romantic attachments were formed in the house on West Grand Boulevard.

Smokey Robinson, a central member of the early Motown family, recalled in his autobiography the relationship between the small but successful group of artists at the time. "Though competition flamed the fire in our hearts," he reminisced, "we also glowed with warm love for each other. Somehow, these two emotions lived side by side. We were rivals and we were friends. . . . We helped each other while trying to top each other."

Diane Ross was 14 years old when Gordy was making his first efforts at running a record company. Although she was still in high school, her mind was already filled with plans for a glamorous career in modeling or singing. When offered an audition with a local quartet calling themselves the Primettes, she jumped at the chance.

The Primettes were initially created as a female counterpart to the Primes, a male trio that would later become the Temptations. The Primes' manager, a flashy Detroit local named Milton Jenkins, decided to build the Primettes around Florence Ballard, a 15-year-old from the Brewster-Douglass Projects whose older sister he was dating. Ballard had a strong, bluesy voice that Jenkins believed would form the ideal backbone for the group. Ballard then recruited her friend and neighbor Mary Wilson, who was a year younger. Wilson had a more fragile but nevertheless lovely voice that nicely complemented Ballard's style.

Ballard and Wilson began rehearsing while they looked for a few other girls to complete their lineup. After several false starts, they ended up with a third singer named Betty McGlown, and Primes member Paul Williams recommended Diane Ross to complete the quartet. When Ross auditioned in the courtyard of the Brewster-Douglass Projects, nearly all the residents gathered to listen. Everyone liked what they heard, and she went inside to rehearse with the band. The four voices blended well, and the Primettes were born.

Success was still several years away at this point, and Ross's position in the group was weakened by her father's utter disapproval. Fred Ross believed that Diane's interest in singing was impractical and a distraction from her studies. He was livid at the idea of his 14-year-old daughter practicing in the hotel suite of manager Milton Jenkins, whom he considered a shady character. But Ernestine Ross, perhaps because of her own love of music, provided Diane with strong encouragement.

Many accounts of Ross's career focus on her father's negative attitude, but Mary Wilson felt that he was not really trying to hold Diane back or control her life. "Unlike many other families then," she recalled, "the Rosses didn't cling to the old idea that the family came before the individual. Instead, they emphasized the importance of each child's personal achievements, and education was considered crucial. Diane always had a streak of daring and independence."

The Temptations, pictured here in 1960, began their career in Detroit as a trio called the Primes. When Diane Ross and her friends formed a singing group in 1958, they called themselves the Primettes, hoping to gain fame as the sister group of the better-known combo.

Even though he had encouraged his daughter to express herself as an individual, Fred Ross still tried to put the brakes on her singing career a number of times over the years. At one point early in the Primettes' career, Diane came down with a bad case of the flu and was out of commission for weeks. Fred sent his daughter Barbara to replace her, in the vague hope that when Diane recovered she would have somehow lost interest in the group and be glad that her older sister had gotten her off the hook. The stratagem failed. When Diane recovered she immediately wanted to continue singing with the Primettes, and Barbara—who was probably most content when she was alone with a book—was only too happy to step down.

Initially, Florence Ballard sang most of the leads for the Primettes, since she had the strongest voice and had been the founding member of the group. The Primettes were soon playing at local record hops, often opening for the Primes. Within a year, the girls had recorded their first single, which featured two songs, "Tears of Sorrow" and "Pretty Baby." Released in March 1959 by a fly-by-night label called Lu-Pine, the record impressed the singers' friends and relatives but did not meet with much success outside of Detroit.

The first big break for the Primettes came on July 4, 1960, when they were asked to perform at the Detroit/Windsor Freedom Festival, a talent show held in Windsor, Ontario (just over the Canadian border from Michigan). The show was scheduled to be broadcast on radio stations in Canada and the United States. Naturally, the trip became a point of contention between Diana and her father, who also happened to be celebrating his 40th birthday on that day.

In the end, Fred Ross agreed to let Diane sing at the festival with the Primettes. The group delivered a tremendous performance and won first place in the competition. Further sweetening their victory, a talent scout from Tamla heard the group and suggested that they try to audition for Berry Gordy back in Detroit. Ecstatic about their good fortune, the Primettes headed back home and began preparing in earnest. With a little prodding from Smokey Robinson, whom Ross was able to contact through some of her old neighborhood acquaintances, the girls soon secured their audition.

The first audition at Motown, however, was a disappointment for the Primettes. As they later recalled, Gordy walked in and out of the room while they sang, scarcely listening. Unknown to them at the time, Gordy's disinterested manner was actually part of his business technique—he never let on that he had anything more than a passing interest in the Primettes or any other performers. In most cases, Gordy got what he wanted; he never had to beg.

Perhaps with a premonition of things to come, the savvy Gordy did perk up his ears when Ross's wispy voice stood out on the group's rendition of the Drifters' "There Goes My Baby." But he told the Primettes quite firmly that they were too young to record for Tamla. Indeed, Ross and Wilson were only 16 at the time, and McGlown, the oldest Primette, was only 18. But as far as the Primettes were concerned, Gordy's remark about their age was just an excuse to get rid of them.

In her autobiography, *Dreamgirl: My Life as a Supreme*, Mary Wilson explained Tamla's reservations. "They didn't feel they could take a chance on another girl group," she remembers. "Their experience with girl groups had been rough." Although they were gaining in popularity, girl groups were thought by many record companies to be a potential liability. What if they went on the road and got hurt? What if they got pregnant? These were considered to be serious concerns in the early 1960s, where a young woman's "reputation" could make or break her singing career, and they may well have played a role in Gordy's initial rejection of the Primettes.

After conferring among themselves outside Hitsville, the four Primettes marched back into the building that day and for many days thereafter. As Ross later put it, "I decided that if Motown was where we wanted to be, why waste time anywhere else?" They were going to make Berry Gordy notice them by being around constantly, even if it took up all their free time. Indeed, such persistence was not unusual for young groups, who spent as much time as they could at Hitsville, soaking up the atmosphere and praying to be given a chance. The Primettes would

The Supremes—(left to right) Mary Wilson, Florence Ballard, and Diane Ross—pose for a photograph during the early 1960s. After struggling for several years to gain recognition, the three youngsters finally convinced Berry Gordy to offer them a recording contract in 1961.

take the bus to Hitsville after school every day and loiter in the reception area until dinner time, jumping at any opportunity to help out around the offices.

Betty McGlown soon tired of this routine, and she quit the Primettes to get married. The three remaining Primettes auditioned a number of other potential singers, finally settling on Barbara Martin, who joined the other members of the group as they continued their vigil in the Tamla offices. Eventually, they were allowed to do backup singing, hand claps, and whatever else was needed for the Tamla recording artists. The four Primettes were paid a small amount to participate in these sessions—just enough to cover their bus fare back and forth to Hitsville.

Despite the low wages and sporadic work, the girls kept coming back, and they quickly became part of the scenery at Hitsville. To their delight, the Primettes were often allowed to sit in and watch other artists record. Even though they were not yet signed to the label, people at least began to know who they were.

Finally, after the Primettes had spent months serving as unofficial office gofers, Gordy relented. He agreed to let them record a song at Hitsville and announced that he was ready to offer them a contract. Later, Ross acknowledged the crucial role Gordy played in her career: "[Berry] demonstrated an undying faith in me. We were a team. . . . For whatever reasons we believed in each other, the end result is the same: He helped me grow and expand my horizons in a larger dream than I ever had for myself."

Between October and December 1960, the Primettes recorded two songs for Gordy, and Ross tried to convince her mother and father to cosign the contract (still underage, she needed the signature of at least one parent). As usual, her father was adamantly opposed to the idea. Aside from the fact that he wanted Diane to finish high school and go to college, he was not convinced that Tamla was a reputable business. If his daughter was bent on pursuing a career in music—an idea to which he was slowly resigning himself—he at least expected the music industry to treat her with the respect he knew she deserved. Finally, exasperated by the whole idea, he decided to let Diane's mother make the decision. If it proved to be the ruin of his daughter's life, he reasoned, at least his signature would not be the one on the fatal contract.

Ernestine Ross and the mothers of the other Primettes went to Hitsville to discuss the arrangements. Impressed by Gordy and his sister Esther Edwards, the company's vice-president in charge of talent management, the four mothers agreed to let their daughters sign up as Tamla artists.

Before he drew up a contract, Gordy was determined to change the group's name. He said he had no idea what a "primette" was supposed to be, and he did not see why his newest vocal group should set themselves up as little more than a sister act to a male group. He pointed out that the Primes no longer existed anyway—they had become the Temptations.

One of Tamla's staff members drew up a list of potential names from which the girls would be allowed to select. Choices included the Darleens, the Sweet P's, the Melodees, the Royaltones, the Jewelettes, and the Supremes. After much arguing over the list of possibilities, the girls decided on the name that would carry them to the fame and glory that Diane Ross had dreamed about for years. The contracts were signed in January 1961, and—two months shy of Diane Ross's 17th birthday—the Supremes were born. •◊•

4

"GET YOURSELF A HIT RECORD"

E VEN THOUGH HER career was already taking off, Ross managed to graduate from high school in January 1962. But by that time, most of her attention was focused on her singing. The Supremes had already released two singles for Tamla; although neither of these first efforts achieved great success, Ross suddenly found herself the center of attention in school and in her neighborhood. Even in the star factory of Hitsville, people were beginning to know who she was. She and the other Supremes were slowly becoming local heroes in Detroit.

Shortly after Ross's graduation, Barbara Martin announced that she was pregnant. She remained with the Supremes for a time, singing with them at local clubs such as the 20 Grand, but eventually left as her pregnancy progressed. Ross, Wilson, and Ballard decided to continue as a trio, and it was this combination of voices that captured the world's attention over the next several years.

Ross fondly recalled the chemistry that made the Supremes click: "Florence was tall, proud, and beautiful, with fair skin and fine hair. She was absolutely regal, and the strength in her voice matched her carriage. [Mary] had a beautiful harmony voice with a great deal of warmth to it. She fit so well with Florence and me; she carried the exact sound just between the two of us that blended all our voices

As the Supremes began to churn out hits during the 1960s, they transformed themselves from a homespun girl group into a trio of glamorous superstars.

41

together, the sound that made up the perfect harmony so that we were like one voice. And Mary had
charisma onstage. She was the sexy one."

For most of 1962, the Supremes did shows around
Detroit, opening for other rhythm and blues acts.
They released another single in May 1962, and later
in the year their career at Tamla really began to take
shape. Gordy was organizing a national tour, the
Motor Town Revue, which would feature many popu-
lar Tamla artists and result in the change of the
company's name to Motown. Such favorites as
Smokey Robinson and the Miracles, the Contours,
Marvin Gaye, Martha and the Vandellas, and the
Marvelettes were scheduled to participate.

The tour would take the artists all across the
country, ending at the famous Apollo Theater in New
York. A group that made a favorable impression on
the boisterous audiences at the Apollo could consider
themselves the crème de la crème of black performers.
"You had to play the Apollo," one performer remembered. "[Then] you had made it."

Initially, Gordy was reluctant to let the Supremes
go on the road. They were the youngest trio at Tamla,
and he was concerned for their well-being among
older artists, particularly male groups like the Contours and the Miracles. In addition, he was worried
about the physical safety of all the performers, largely
because the tour included an extended jaunt through
the South, the epicenter of the explosive civil rights
movement and still a hotbed of racial strife. But the
persistent Supremes won Gordy over, and they were
put on the bill. Since they lacked a big hit record,
they were scheduled to be the opening act.

In the South, Ross saw incidents of racism she
had never dreamed of as a young child staying with
her grandparents in Alabama. The tour group, most
of them traveling in a large bus, were denied service
in restaurants and gas stations, and several confron-

tations nearly escalated into lethal violence as white racists took extreme measures to keep the black performers out of their establishments. Once, in Birmingham, Alabama, the members of the Motown tour were shot at as they loaded up their bus following a show. Luckily, everyone was able to get on board and leave town unharmed, but the bullet holes in the window became a reminder that racism remained a serious problem in America.

Yet even gunfire and racial turmoil could not dampen Ross's spirits. In the southern theaters, which were mostly segregated with white patrons on one side and black patrons on the other, she stood dead center on the stage, singing earnestly to everyone. "Did these incidents have any influence on my life?" she later reflected. "I'm sure they did, but they did not change my love and respect for humanity and did not make me judge the white friends and associates I had. I found that there are wonderful, decent people and mean, bad people in both the black and white worlds."

Despite all the difficulties, the tour was an unparalleled success. The Supremes were not headliners like some of the other groups who had already put out hit records, but audiences both black and white responded well to their sweet, melodic pop sound. To cap off their experience, the Supremes played for 10 nights at the Apollo Theater before returning to Detroit in December.

One seemingly minor incident during the Apollo engagement remained fixed in Ross's memory. At the Apollo shows, there was usually an emcee who appeared onstage between acts and urged the audience to give the departing performers a round of applause. But after the Supremes opened the bill on the first night, the Apollo emcee decided not to waste his energy on these unknown youngsters, and he stayed in the wings. The comedian Scoey Mitchell, who

The first great event in the Supremes' career was a 1962 cross-country Motown tour that ended at Harlem's Apollo Theater. During the 10-night engagement, the young singers had to win over the Apollo's demanding patrons, who could be brutal to performers they disliked.

came on right after the Supremes, did the honors on the first night but was determined not to do it again—after all, it was not his job. So the following night, when the Supremes finished their set, no one urged the audience to show any appreciation. There was only mild applause, and the Supremes shuffled off the stage, confused and embarrassed.

Ross was furious at Mitchell for leaving the Supremes in such an uncomfortable spot in front of the large, hard-to-please Apollo audience, and she told him what she thought of him. Mitchell snapped back: "I tell you what, little girl. You better stop fussing with me and go and try and get yourself a hit record." Apparently the comment made quite an impression on Ross. Before long she and the Supremes reached heights none of them could ever have expected.

By the beginning of 1963, Gordy had begun to see the Supremes as more than just a second-tier act on his star-studded roster. Eddie and Brian Holland and Lamont Dozier, Motown's best songwriting team, were put to work making hits for the Supremes, as they had for the Marvelettes and Martha and the Vandellas. In October 1963, the Supremes had some success with the single "When the Lovelight Starts Shining Through His Eyes," which made the top 100 on the rhythm and blues charts.

Gordy also decided that Ross should sing all of the leads for the group. Her voice was the most unconventional and distinctive of the three; its earnest, nasal quality would make the group instantly identifiable. Although Florence and Mary still hoped to sing some leads, they were willing to go along with Gordy's decision if it would make them famous. They were all too aware of Gordy's formidable instinct for making hits, and if he thought Diana's voice should stand out, then they were ready to fade into the background.

Soon after Gordy made his crucial decision, the Holland-Dozier-Holland team came up with the song that would propel the Supremes into the big time once and for all. Originally written with the already-popular Marvelettes in mind, "Where Did Our Love Go?" was handed over to the Supremes when the Marvelettes turned it down. Wanda Rogers, one of the Marvelettes, proclaimed that the song was "the most pitiful tune we'd ever heard."

The Supremes recorded the song reluctantly at first because they were not happy about being stuck with someone else's leftovers. As per Gordy's request, Ross sang lead on the song. In a moment of inspiration, the Holland-Dozier-Holland production team dropped the key of the song by slowing down the tape, giving Ross's voice a sultrier, more mature edge.

When the record was actually released in June 1964, the Supremes were already on their second national tour, along with Dick Clark's "Cavalcade of Stars," which featured Gene Pitney, the Shirelles, and other successful acts. Before the record hit the airwaves, they were near the bottom of the bill. But around the middle of June, "Where Did Our Love Go?" shot to the top of the charts with dizzying speed. A month into the tour, the song had gone to number one and was receiving more radio airplay than any other record.

Years later, an article in *Time* magazine recalled the resonance of the song at the time it was released. "Florence and Mary sang in the background, while Ross did the lead in a voice that was equal parts coyness, sexiness, nicotine, and velvet. 'Baby, baby, where did our love go?' they purred, and that little question sent them right to the top."

As the "Cavalcade of Stars" tour progressed, the Supremes were boosted to the top of the bill. Ross and her fellow Supremes could not believe the suddenness of the turnaround. Instead of receiving only polite applause when they played outside of Detroit, the Supremes were now greeted with screams of approval from their young audiences. With one explosive hit, they had become stars—not just on the rhythm and blues charts but also on the pop charts, the traditional domain of white listeners.

The Supremes were not the only ones overwhelmed with joy. Their success was also a dream come true for Berry Gordy. For five years he had been turning out popular music by black artists, but the records rarely garnered attention from white audiences. Gordy had been striving for a "crossover" hit since the inception of Tamla. Now young people from all ethnic backgrounds were rushing to the stores to pick up "Where Did Our Love Go?"

While the Supremes finished their national tour, Gordy was busy in Detroit getting ready for their return. Most important, he decided that the Holland-Dozier-Holland team would now concentrate all of their time and energy writing songs for the Supremes. The talented songwriters rapidly crafted two new songs, "Baby Love" and "Come See About Me," which the Supremes recorded upon their return to Detroit. In the fall of 1964, both songs shot up the pop charts to number one.

The group then put out an album entitled *Where Did Our Love Go?* featuring their three hit singles plus a number of other tunes. The album sold close to 1 million copies and remained on the pop charts for

The Supremes disembark at London's Heathrow Airport in October 1964, prior to beginning a European tour. At the time, the group's first two hit records, "Where Did Our Love Go?" and "Baby Love," were topping the charts on both sides of the Atlantic.

over a year. At this point, even the pessimistic Fred Ross would have been hard-pressed to deny that his daughter was becoming a huge success.

For the rest of the year, the Supremes jetted around the United States and Europe, capitalizing on their newfound stardom. They spent a full two weeks touring Great Britain, during which they performed on the British television show "Thank Your Lucky Stars." Mary Wilson recalled the warm surprise the group received when they first stepped off the plane in England and were greeted by dozens of members of the Tamla-Motown Appreciation Society. British fans were quite familiar with the Supremes by this time. Aside from "Baby Love," only one other record by an American artist—Roy Orbison's "It's Over"— had hit number one in Britain in 1964.

British journalists could not get enough of America's newest singing sensation, and the Supremes were constantly in the spotlight. As Wilson recalled, "We were asked our opinions on everything from the British music invasion to fashion." In England, the Supremes also had a chance to meet Ringo Starr and Paul McCartney, two members of the Beatles, who were also well on the way to world fame.

The excitement of the British tour led to the second Supremes album, *A Bit of Liverpool*, on which they tried their hand at popular British songs of the day. After finishing that recording, their jet-setting lifestyle took them to Los Angeles to appear in the Teen-Age Music International Show, where they were billed alongside such acts as the Beach Boys, the Rolling Stones, Marvin Gaye, Jan and Dean, Chuck Berry, and James Brown.

The Supremes also took a trip to Hollywood, where they filmed a movie called *Bikini Party*, which was never released. While there, however, they were thrilled to have the opportunity to meet Sidney

Poitier, who for many years had been the most popular and respected black film actor in America.

The most exciting moment for the Supremes came on December 27, 1964. On that date, they appeared live on "The Ed Sullivan Show," the most popular television variety show of the day, watched by millions of Americans every Sunday evening. The Supremes were the first Motown act to be featured by Sullivan. Wearing blue dresses, they sang "Come See About Me" to an enthusiastic studio audience, making countless new fans across the nation and achieving a major advance for black music.

One of the oddest stories regarding the group emerged during the Sullivan telecast. Because there had been so few black performers on the show, the makeup artists were not sure how to handle them. After the artists' first try, the three singers resembled, as Mary Wilson recalled, "black-faced singers in a minstrel show." Horrified at their image in the mirror, the Supremes rapidly removed all the makeup and did the job themselves.

The Supremes' appearance on "The Ed Sullivan Show" confirmed what most of Detroit already knew: there were three superstars in their midst—at least when they were not busy touring the world. The Rosses suddenly found themselves the most sought-after family in town. Party invitations poured in for the children, and Fred and Ernestine had trouble walking down the street without being stopped at every corner by a dedicated Supremes fan who wanted to meet the rest of Motown's first family.

Other members of Motown's larger musical family found that the "crossover" success of the Supremes was helping to introduce their own material to broader, multiracial audiences. In a 1965 article, *Newsweek* reported that of the 60 singles Motown had released during the previous year, 42 had been hits,

The Supremes' appearances on TV's "Ed Sullivan Show" brought them to the attention of a nationwide audience. As this photo suggests, Diana Ross was steadily emerging as the dominant member of the trio.

selling a total of 12 million copies and bringing the company $10 million in revenue.

The Supremes' hit records, along with their appearance on "The Ed Sullivan Show," had given Motown the exposure it needed to turn itself into a truly national label. By the end of 1964, Motown was putting out the most consistently high-quality pop music of any label in the country. The record-buying public was clearly more interested in the content of the records than in the skin color of the people who were making them. At this point, the artificial distinction between "black music" and "white music" was largely irrelevant.

When the Supremes were in Detroit on their rare breaks from out-of-town concerts and publicity events, a team of "charm school" instructors—officially called Motown Artist Development—was working overtime on the group, who were quickly becoming the label's top act. In addition to voice and dance lessons, the Supremes went to etiquette classes that taught them everything from the proper way to curtsy (necessary for meetings with royalty) to which type of flatware to use at the dinner table. As Wilson recalled, the singers were constantly under scrutiny: "Were my shoulders straight? Was my posture good? Was my makeup—the little I wore then—feminine and flattering—not too brassy? Which fork to use, how to greet people, how to hold eating utensils, how to enter a room, how to find a chair, and how to sit and rise gracefully were all part of the program."

Not surprisingly, Ross proved to be the most ambitious of the three in all of the classes. In many ways, she had been distinguishing herself as the central figure in the Supremes for some time. For instance, after the three singers would agree on matching stage dress for a given show, Ross would show up wearing something completely different in order to put herself in the spotlight. And while Ballard and Wilson may have complained about their partner's relentless ambition to be the star of the show, neither they nor anyone else could deny that Ross worked harder than either of the other Supremes.

For the time being, rivalry was overshadowed by success. The Supremes were all riding high, unable to believe the good fortune that had given them three number one hits in a single year. But the best was still to come. ◖◗

5

MOVIN' ON UP

❧

BEFORE THE SUPREMES could catch their breath after their whirlwind of success, they were back in the studio on January 5, 1965, to record what was to become their fourth number one hit, "Stop! in the Name of Love." The song had been inspired by an argument between songwriter Lamont Dozier and his wife. In the middle of the dispute, Dozier had come up with the ridiculous line; both he and his wife began to laugh, and a hit was born. In March, the song climbed above the Beatles' "Eight Days a Week" to the pinnacle of the pop charts. It was an auspicious beginning to what promised to be another busy year.

During the course of the year, the Supremes appeared on more than 15 national television shows. In addition to many more appearances on "The Ed Sullivan Show" (Sullivan grew to love the group), the Supremes were featured on "Hullabaloo," "The Hollywood Palace," "The Tonight Show," "The Dean Martin Show," and "The Red Skelton Show," to name just a few. Suddenly, they were familiar faces among the top stars of stage and screen. They were seen on television with Sammy Davis, Jr., Bob Newhart, and Judy Garland, and they also appeared on the covers of *Time* and *Ebony* magazines.

That year, during the *Gemini V* space flight, the mission control crew played "Where Did Our Love

A glittering Ross accompanies Berry Gordy and his son Berry IV to a gala event at the Coconut Grove in Los Angeles in 1969. By this time, Gordy had become the dominant figure in Ross's life, both professionally and personally.

Go?" for the astronauts as they orbited the earth, taking the Supremes all the way to outer space. But perhaps their endorsement of Coca-Cola, often considered as symbolic of America as the Stars and Stripes, truly indicated that the Supremes had made it to the top.

The Supremes embarked upon another European tour in 1965. The tour was sponsored by Motown and featured many of the same acts that had participated on the earlier Motor Town Revue, along with the newest young singing sensation, Stevie Wonder. The Motown artists visited most of the major cities in Western Europe, including London, Paris, and Hamburg. Although crowds in Europe did not attend in record numbers—the Supremes were the only group on the tour that most Europeans were familiar with—the critics raved about these memorable shows. Regarding the tour's poor reception in England, one British critic wrote, "We are forced to the following conclusion that English audiences are either stone deaf or cabbages in disguise. How live human beings could sit through that talent-loaded show and not be moved escapes us!" Indeed, Motown had reached a pinnacle with their host of talented artists, and the Supremes were the centerpiece.

Ross's voice continued to be the single most marketable asset Motown possessed. It had a quality that everyone responded to but few could pin down. The well-known African-American novelist Jamaica Kincaid may have come closest when she remembered listening to the Supremes when she was growing up in the 1960s: "No girl anywhere has ever sounded like that. It was the voice of a young girl wanting everything yet not knowing what it was that she wanted or what it was that she would get."

During the 1965 European tour, the Supremes began using their most famous choreographic move. At the last minute before filming an important

The Supremes demonstrate their best-known dance move while performing "Stop! in the Name of Love," which became their fourth number one hit.

BBC-TV special in London, Ross became frantic because the group had no distinctive moves for "Stop! in the Name of Love." Reportedly, she burst into the men's dressing room, where the Temptations were getting ready for the show, and pleaded for help. On the spur of the moment, one of the Temptations had the clever idea of using a palm-out, police-style "Stop!" gesture, a move that would become a Supremes trademark. Thirty years later, most listeners— even the younger generations who may never have seen the Supremes—are inclined to repeat this gesture when the song comes on the radio.

Around this time, rumors of a love interest between Ross and Berry Gordy were confirmed. Long before the tour began, speculation around the Motown offices suggested that the two were either romantically involved or at least headed in that direction, but neither party would offer any confirmation. On the tour, however, Ross confided to Ballard and Wilson that she and Gordy had begun dating.

Ross's relationship with Gordy, which lasted many years, would be central to her career. Even after they stopped dating, the two remained close friends and business associates. Perhaps more than any other Motown artist, Ross had a great deal of control over the direction of her career and that of the Supremes.

The big event of 1965, looming above all their other appearances and recordings, was the Supremes' scheduled appearances at New York's swank nightclub the Copacabana (popularized later in a Barry Manilow song). Although their Copacabana dates were not scheduled until July, they began rehearsing in earnest months in advance. In 1965, only the top acts performed at the world-renowned supper club—Frank Sinatra was frequently featured—and the audiences invariably included the biggest luminaries in show business.

Shows at the Copacabana were classy affairs, not wild concerts packed with screaming teenagers. In fact, rock and roll groups were rarely featured at the club because they did not attract the kind of crowds the Copacabana wanted. For the Supremes, this involved a change in emphasis. They began intensive training to create a theatrical masterpiece, with flashy dance routines and a well-orchestrated musical set.

All three of the Supremes took classes with professional model Maxine Powell, musical director Maurice King, and renowned choreographer Cholly Atkins, who was working with Gladys Knight and the Pips at the time. Ross took extra courses in modeling and makeup at Detroit's famed John Robert Powers School for Social Grace in preparation for the Copacabana shows. Success in the new venue meant a great deal to the Supremes. If they were a hit at the

Copacabana, it would show that they were more than just a teenage phenomenon and that they could attract older, more sophisticated audiences as well.

On a sweltering evening in late July 1965, the Supremes played their first show in front of a packed house at the Copacabana. In attendance that night were Ed Sullivan, boxer Joe Louis, and ubiquitous man-about-town Sammy Davis, Jr., among others. The weeks of preparation paid off, and the show was a phenomenal success. Closing their set with "You're Nobody Till Someone Loves You," the Supremes brought the audience to their feet with cries of "More! More!" Watching Ross perform that evening, Berry Gordy probably started thinking about her solo career.

Aside from their triumphant appearance at the Copacabana, the Supremes were achieving hit after hit with their records. Following the incredible success of "Stop! in the Name of Love," there were more and more hits, including "Back in My Arms Again," "Nothing but Heartaches," "I Hear a Symphony," and "My World Is Empty Without You." The album *The Supremes A-Go-Go*, released the following year, deposed the Beatles' album *Revolver* at the number one spot on the pop charts and became the Supremes' first number one album.

Over the course of 1965, the Supremes consistently remained on both the pop and rhythm and blues charts, and after their shows at the Copacabana, the range of their listenership expanded even more. At this point, anyone from Ed Sullivan to a starstruck teenager might comfortably spin a Supremes record.

In the summer of 1965, just a few months after Ross's 21st birthday, Berry Gordy bought a house for each of the Supremes on Detroit's Buena Vista Street, located in a comfortable middle-class neighborhood. Mary Wilson bought a second house in the same neighborhood to accommodate her mother and fam-

The Beatles, shown here with TV host Ed Sullivan, battled the Supremes for the number one spot on the pop charts during the mid-1960s. The groups met in 1965, with disappointing results: the Supremes found the Beatles scruffy and unglamorous, while the British rockers considered the Supremes totally conventional.

ily. Ross's mother and sisters moved into her new house, which was usually unoccupied because Ross now spent most of her time on the road. The Supremes were finally leaving behind the housing projects for good at a time when life in Detroit's inner city was becoming increasingly dangerous.

While the Supremes were in New York in August for another appearance on "The Ed Sullivan Show," they had an odd encounter with the Beatles, who were staying at the same hotel. Though they professed to be great fans of the Supremes and the Motown sound in general, the Beatles gave the Supremes a rather cool reception. Dressed, as Mary Wilson recalled, in "elegant day dresses, hats, gloves, high heels, and jewelry," the Supremes went to pay a visit at the Beatles' suite, probably expecting to meet the four clean-cut "mop tops" that the British quartet's public persona suggested. Instead, they found the Beatles' suite reeking of marijuana smoke and discovered that John, Paul, George, and Ringo were all dressed quite shabbily. After several awkward attempts at conversation, the Supremes left. For their part, the Beatles had also expected something quite different in the girl group that was storming the pop charts. As George Harrison later confessed, "We expected soulful, hip girls. We couldn't believe that three black girls from Detroit could be so square!"

Indeed, with all of their charm school training—plus a healthy dose of natural innocence—the Supremes had cultivated a clean-cut image. This was part of the reason why sophisticated audiences, such as those attending the Copacabana, could enjoy the group as much as the teenage pop fans who had first brought them into the limelight.

In October 1965, the Supremes returned to New York to play before another packed house at Philharmonic Hall in Lincoln Center. The first pop group to perform at a venue usually reserved for classical music, they remembered the show as one of their finest. In November they played Madison Square Garden, where they appeared alongside Sammy Davis, Jr., Johnny Carson, Joan Crawford, and other show business legends. Their string of hit singles continued, and when they were not on the road they were busy in the recording studio at Motown. Because they had become quite popular all over Europe, the group found themselves rerecording their songs in such foreign languages as German, French, and Spanish.

In January 1966, Ross officially announced that from then on she would be known as Diana, the name on her birth certificate, rather than Diane. Although this pronouncement may not have been earthshaking at the time, it was a signal that Ross was beginning to distance herself from the other two Supremes.

By this time, trouble was beginning to brew among the group members. Although Mary Wilson continued to work hard, Florence Ballard began skipping rehearsals and failing to appear at recording sessions. In March 1966, when the group was booked at the Copacabana, Ballard complained of flu symptoms; Ross and Wilson flirted with the idea of replacing her, at least for the week-long engagement. In the end, Ballard went onstage, but her erratic behavior suggested that something was bothering her. Considering the constant pressure the three young women were under to perform and to be on their best behavior even off the stage, it was certainly understandable that such intensity might wear heavily on their spirits.

Even Ross, unquestionably the most strong-willed member of the group, showed signs of strain. At one show in Boston that March, she became seriously distraught and had to be escorted off the stage. Ross recovered quickly and was soon back to the hectic schedule of shows, interviews, and recording sessions that kept the Supremes in the limelight. They were still at the top of their form, and the bouncy, infectious "You Can't Hurry Love" brought the group another massive hit in July 1966. Along with "Where Did Our Love Go?" this song was a million-seller almost overnight.

In September 1966, the Supremes toured the Far East, playing in Tokyo, Taiwan, Hong Kong, Manila, and at a number of United States military bases. With the war in Vietnam increasing in scope, many wounded U.S. soldiers were being sent to Japan for medical treatment. The Supremes were deeply saddened by the tragedy of the war, but they managed to remain cheerful enough to perform for the veterans they met. These visits had special resonance for Diana, as her younger brother Fred junior had gone to fight in Vietnam.

Throughout Asia, the Supremes found themselves the center of attention everywhere they went—both because of their phenomenal popularity

The Supremes pose for a photo with Berry Gordy, Motown executive Esther Edwards (left), and a pair of geishas during a 1966 visit to Japan. The group's Far East tour, which included Hong Kong, Taiwan, and the Philippines, confirmed their standing as international superstars.

and because, quite simply, most Asians had never seen African-American women before. Indeed, the Supremes' global success was scarcely equaled by any of the other Motown groups.

Later in September, the group performed once again on "The Ed Sullivan Show," singing a tune from their soon-to-be-released Christmas album. Four days later, the Supremes flew to Las Vegas for a series of shows at the Flamingo Hotel. Back in Detroit, as 1966 came to a close, they began working on an album of Rodgers and Hart show tunes. More than any other Motown group—in fact, more than almost any other pop group—the Supremes had clearly gone beyond the limits of pop music.

But through all of this success, it became clearer each day that Florence Ballard was unhappy and wanted to leave the group. In April 1967, the three Supremes held a meeting to discuss the situation. Interviewed several years later, Ross vividly remembered the day's events: "We had a talk with Flo and her mother and wanted to find out if leaving the group was really her final decision. And that was really what she wanted to do. She had made up her mind. She felt it just wasn't the right thing for her." As the other former members of the Supremes and the Primettes could have pointed out, a career in music is not for everyone.

A tearful good-bye followed in April, made particularly sad since the three had recently finished recording several songs that would all go on to be major hits: "The Happening," "Reflections," and "In and Out of Love." Ross, Wilson, and Ballard had been performing together for nearly eight years, but it was clearly time for a change. ◖◗

6

"SAY IT LOUD"

To REPLACE FLORENCE BALLARD, the Supremes chose Cindy Birdsong, who had been singing backup vocals with Patti LaBelle and the Bluebelles. Birdsong quickly proved to be a fine singer and performer. Just two days after she was hired, the Supremes were able to put on an excellent performance at the Hollywood Bowl, a benefit for the United Negro College Fund.

Other changes were in the works as well, as it became more and more obvious that Diana Ross was the real star of the group. Soon after Ballard left, Gordy decided that the name of the trio should be changed to Diana Ross and the Supremes. By this point, Ross was the clear celebrity of the trio. She was the one reporters called upon to interview, the one who sang the leads and gave the Supremes their distinctive sound. Hers was the voice that had catapulted them to the top of the charts and kept them there. As in the case of Smokey Robinson and the Miracles, Ross's name out front would only add to the drawing power of the already successful group.

Ross relaxes on the balcony of her Beverly Hills home in 1971. After leaving the Supremes in 1969, the singing star moved to California in order to pursue her career as a solo performer and film actress.

Inevitably, there was some resentment of Ross's superstar status among her fellow Supremes and among other female performers at Motown. But, as Smokey Robinson pointed out, "What's most evident is that Diana's remarkable abilities as an entertainer kicked her up into another category. She demanded that attention; she earned it. She had the charisma to fill football stadiums all over the world."

Due to circumstances unrelated to Ballard's departure or Ross's promotion in the Supremes, Motown lost the services of Holland-Dozier-Holland around this same time, as the three talented songwriters went on to try their hand at independent production. All in all, 1967 turned out to be a difficult year for Diana Ross and the Supremes, with a new member to train and the loss of a top-notch production team.

As ambitious as ever, Ross began to branch out into other areas of show business. Always interested in acting, she landed her first role in 1967, appearing as a guest star on an episode of the popular television series "Tarzan." She and the two other Supremes played the role of three nuns, wearing black habits and singing "Michael Row the Boat Ashore" and "The Lord Helps Those Who Help Themselves." The popular African-American actor James Earl Jones also appeared in the episode, which aired the following January.

By the beginning of 1968, Diana Ross and the Supremes had resumed their jet-setting schedule. The year began with a European tour, including concerts in Stockholm, Madrid, Paris, and London. As usual, the European critics raved about the group. While abroad, they were introduced to such British celebrities as Tom Jones, Mick Jagger, Vanessa Redgrave, Marianne Faithfull, and Brian Jones. The Supremes were even given a private audience with the Duke and Duchess of Bedford, members of the British royal family, who invited them to their estate, Woburn

Abbey. They had certainly come a long way from the Detroit housing projects.

When the Supremes returned home, they found more excitement, but of a much graver nature. While they were performing at the Copacabana in early April, civil rights leader Martin Luther King, Jr., was assassinated in Memphis. It was a difficult time for all Americans, and as African-American performers who had seen American racism at its worst, the Supremes were deeply saddened.

Asked to perform in memory of Dr. King on "The Tonight Show," Ross worked hard with Berry Gordy to create a heartfelt tribute to the great leader. They decided that the popular Supremes song "Somewhere," which featured a spoken-word part in the middle, would serve as the centerpiece of the performance. Instead of the usual words about love and romance, however, Ross invoked Dr. King's name

The coffin of Dr. Martin Luther King, Jr., makes its way along an Atlanta street in April 1968. Like most Americans, Ross was deeply shaken by the brutal murder of the great civil rights leader, and she began to incorporate Dr. King's words into her performances.

and recited a section from his best-remembered "I Have a Dream" speech. Afterward, when she was interviewed by Carson, she expressed her deep appreciation for King's work, saying, "I know he lived and died for one reason—and I want all of us to be together."

The tribute to Dr. King soon became a standby of Supremes shows, and it often moved their audiences to tears. President Lyndon Johnson saw the Supremes perform in Los Angeles and later came backstage to speak with Ross. With great emotion, he assured her that he would do everything possible to see that Dr. King's dream became a reality. "It's going to happen," Johnson assured the singer. "Little by little, we're getting there."

In keeping with the highly politicized tenor of the late 1960s, Diana Ross and the Supremes continued to support those causes they found important. At the request of Coretta Scott King, Dr. King's widow, they and a number of other popular Motown artists performed at a concert in Atlanta to benefit the Poor People's Campaign. Later that year, they began working on the enormous hit "Love Child," a song that addressed the problem of illegitimate children, which was becoming a serious issue in the age of sexual revolution. In what was now almost a tradition, "Love Child" pushed a Beatles tune, "Hey Jude," out of the number one spot on the pop charts. One can only wonder how the British rockers felt about this "square" group from Detroit that consistently topped them on the charts.

By the end of 1968, Diana Ross and the Supremes were back in Europe, touring to promote their new hit. At their show in London, the entire British royal family, including Queen Elizabeth and the young Prince Charles, attended the show. Closing the set with "Somewhere," Ross once again improvised on a well-known phrase from one of Martin Luther King,

Jr.'s great speeches. "Free at last!" she intoned, her arms stretched out to the audience. "Free at last! Free at last!" At the close of the number, the entire audience jumped to their feet for an emotion-filled standing ovation.

Although the royal family were among the first ones out of their chairs for the standing ovation, the British press initially chastised Ross for what they considered to be disrespectful behavior. Broaching the political issue of racism and civil rights in the esteemed presence of British royalty was not considered proper etiquette. But Ross refused to back down from her stance, quoting the energetic African-American performer James Brown, whose popular song ran "Say it loud . . . I'm black and I'm proud!"

As the year came to a close, the Supremes scored another hit when they collaborated with the Temptations on "I'm Gonna Make You Love Me." After recording the song, the two high-powered groups began preparing for a joint network television special. The show was called "T.C.B.—Taking Care of Business" (an expression that Elvis Presley would later adopt as his motto). It was to feature an eye-catching, futuristic stage set and a number of medleys featuring the Supremes and the Temptations.

Beginning years before as the Primes and the Primettes, the two had risen from brother and sister acts on the streets of Detroit to wildly successful performers on an international scale. "T.C.B." was the culmination of years of hard work and a celebration of both groups' achievements. Not surprisingly, the show was enthusiastically received by critics and audiences, and it provided another showcase for Ross's versatile singing, dancing, and acting talents.

In the summer of 1969, Ross demonstrated her interest in other artists when she helped to bring a hot new singing group to national attention. Known as the Jackson Five, the quintet consisted of five

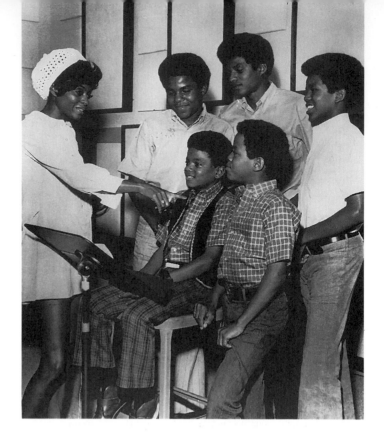

Ross poses with the Jackson Five in 1970. Ross not only helped the talented performers gain national recognition; she also became a surrogate mother to the youngest of the Jackson brothers, Michael (in vest).

youngsters from Gary, Indiana, who would go on to be extremely popular Motown artists, beginning their career with four number one records in a row. After meeting the five youngsters, who had been all but unknown up to that point, Ross found them so endearing that she decided to throw a party for them at the Daisy Club in Hollywood, where she introduced them to the press and to top show-business executives.

At the gala affair, 10-year-old Michael Jackson, the youngest member of the group, stood before a captivated audience and expressed his appreciation to Ross for taking the Jackson Five under her wing. "I had just about given up hope," he told the gathered crowd. "I thought I was going to be an old man before being discovered, but along came Miss Diana Ross to save my career."

Ross continued to promote the group, and their first album had the advantage of bearing the title

Diana Ross Presents the Jackson Five. Later, in the early 1970s, Ross became something of a surrogate mother to young Michael when he came to Los Angeles and lived at her Beverly Hills mansion. Indeed, the two would become lifelong friends as a result of these early gestures.

As 1969 wore on, it became clear that Ross was destined to leave the Supremes and carve out her career as a solo artist. Her fame had eclipsed that of her fellow Supremes, and it was no secret that they had begun to resent her success. Rumors about a breakup had been floating around for several years, but the trio had remained wildly popular, and it was difficult for Ross to part ways with the combo that she had been performing with for a decade—a group that had whisked its way through 12 number one pop songs in the space of five years. Beyond the security provided by the group's hit-making potential, the Supremes and their associates were close friends; despite the turbulence within the group, Ross would find it painful to leave.

But leave she did. The first announcement was made in November 1969, as Motown began to hatch plans for Ross's solo act and to seek a replacement so that the Supremes could continue without her. It was a heartrending time for all involved, but the group pulled together to make a final appearance on "The Ed Sullivan Show" (their 12th in five years) in December. Then they geared up for their final live performance on January 14, 1970, at Las Vegas's swank Frontier Hotel. The last single by Diana Ross and the Supremes, the uplifting spiritual "Someday We'll Be Together," was to be introduced at the Frontier.

Ross recalled the sadness she felt as she prepared for that last show, "applying my makeup, fixing my hair, with a huge lump in my throat and a sting in

After Ross left the Supremes in 1969, the group carried on with a revamped lineup: (left to right) Cindy Birdsong, Mary Wilson, and Jean Terrell.

my nose. I kept pushing the tears down, trying to swallow, holding on to myself so that I wouldn't break apart."

Ross, Wilson, and Birdsong emerged onstage to a roar of approval so loud, Mary Wilson remembered, that "the floor vibrated under my feet like an electric charge." Beginning with a medley of hits including "Baby Love," "Stop! in the Name of Love," "Come

See About Me," and "I Hear a Symphony," the group gave a truly magnificent performance that night. Ross sang solo on a number of the songs, including "I'm Gonna Make You Love Me" and "Didn't We?"

But the highlight of the group's final show was the rousing rendition of "Let the Sunshine In," during which Ross spontaneously walked through the audience, handing the microphone around so that everyone could join in. Motowners such as Smokey Robinson and Marvin Gaye, members of Berry Gordy's family, and such celebrities as Steve Allen and Dick Clark all sang along until the whole audience was on its feet in one great wave of energy, chanting the chorus, "Let the sunshine in," over and over again.

The show closed with the new hit, "Someday We'll Be Together," and finally, "The Impossible Dream." But what may have seemed impossible in 1959 was now a reality. The audience gave the group three standing ovations, and telegrams from Ed Sullivan and the mayor of Las Vegas were read aloud. There were many tearful good-byes, as Berry Gordy mounted the stage to bid farewell to the trio that had helped to put Motown on the map. Finally, Jean Terrell, the new lead singer for the Supremes, was introduced.

And then it was all over. Just three months shy of her 26th birthday, Diana Ross was on her own. ❦

7

DOING IT HERSELF

❧

Ross stars as Billie Holiday in the 1972 film Lady Sings the Blues. *In order to prepare for the demanding role, Ross spent hours listening to Holiday's recordings and speaking to people who had known the brilliant jazz singer.*

As DIANA ROSS eased into her new role as a solo star, she began to make many other changes in her life as well. Early in 1970, she bought a house in Beverly Hills, California, and made this her primary residence, leaving the icy winters of Detroit behind for good. She was beginning to think about extending her career into other areas of show business, such as motion pictures, and the relocation put her closer to the movers and shakers of Hollywood. Around the same time, Motown Records relocated its central offices to Los Angeles.

Motown's hot new production team of Nickolas Ashford and Valerie Simpson began work on Ross's first solo single, eventually coming up with "Reach Out and Touch (Somebody's Hand)." The song, Ross told reporters, spoke to an ever-increasing drug abuse problem among America's young people. Having been back to Detroit to visit her old home in the Brewster Projects, Ross had been shocked at how the area had gone to seed. She wanted to send the message that there was always a helping hand, even in times of great despair where drugs seem to be a temporary solution.

"Reach Out and Touch (Somebody's Hand)" became a favorite at Ross's electrifying concerts for years to come, even if it did not fare so well on the charts. It unified the most disparate audiences, and many concertgoers remember holding hands and singing along with people they had never met before, as a feeling of brotherly and sisterly love washed over them.

Raynoma Gordy Singleton, a relative of Berry Gordy's, recalled the utter magic of Ross's solo shows: "Her performances were executed to perfection, with unparalleled timing, gestures, and expressions. During 'Reach Out and Touch (Somebody's Hand),' with the audience holding hands, swaying, and singing along, Ross floated among them with a follow spot behind. The light was like a halo behind her as she spread stardust kisses on the audience and blessed them with her smiles. No one could pull it off like she could."

Ross's second solo single, "Ain't No Mountain High Enough," enjoyed substantial chart success and also became a popular standby of her live performances. With its rousing gospel feel and chorus of joyful voices, the song shot to number one on the pop charts and was nominated for a Grammy Award. An article in *Rolling Stone* magazine proclaimed the song "one of the ten best singles ever made."

When Ross's fans saw the cover of her debut album, *Diana Ross*, they were surprised to see the singer without her usual glamorous stagewear and heavy makeup. Instead, she appeared barefoot, wearing cutoff jeans and a T-shirt, seemingly at her most vulnerable. She seemed to be telling her fans, "Here I am, without any disguises." Audiences were taken by this new image of Diana Ross, and soon the singer who had wryly announced her first solo shows by saying "Welcome to the 'Let's-See-If-Diana-Ross-Can-Do-It-By-Herself' Show" was proving that she could indeed make it on her own. A critic for the influential show-business magazine *Variety* called Ross a "total entertainer," a "wide-eyed, funny, hip, and endearing street gamin with great vitality, confidence, and presence."

In April 1971, Ross made her first solo television appearance. The hour-long special featured some of her latest songs along with some inspired acting segments in which she tried her hand at doing impressions of W. C. Fields, Harpo Marx, Charlie Chaplin, and other early film stars. Her talents as an actress were becoming evident, and film director Sidney Furie contacted her about the possibility of starring in a new film about the life of the gifted and tragic jazz and blues singer Billie Holiday. The film was to be called *Lady Sings the Blues*. Ross was to play alongside the popular black actor Billy Dee Williams and the versatile comedian Richard Pryor.

For months, Ross worked hard to acquaint herself with the life and music of Holiday, all the while brushing off the remarks of those who doubted her ability to portray the character properly. Some critics claimed that Ross could not play the role because she had not lived the harrowing life of Billie Holiday. Others pointed out that Ross did not look anything like Holiday or harped on the difference between Ross's and Holiday's singing styles. It was clear that many critics considered Ross only a lightweight pop singer, and they were convinced that she was going to offer a cheap Hollywood portrayal of a truly great American artist. The criticism went on and on, long before anyone had so much as a glimpse of the movie.

Undaunted, Ross studied Holiday's music, listening to the records every night for months and immersing herself in the singer's haunting, smoky voice. She pored over photographs and interviewed people who had known Holiday personally. She sat for hours in a reconstruction of Holiday's bedroom and dressing room, trying to capture the aura of the great performer. On the double album that was released prior to the film's opening, Ross proved to critics just how well she had absorbed Holiday's style. The songs were not imitations but skillful renditions that conveyed the vocal intensity and emotional depth of Holiday's performances. The album reached number one (a surprising feat for a collection of jazz and blues songs) and sold 300,000 copies within eight days of its release.

As for Ross's dramatic portrayal of Holiday, Billy Dee Williams—one of the many that had been skeptical of her acting ability—was perhaps in the best position to judge. In a 1973 article, *Rolling Stone* reporter Michael Thomas recounted the moment when Williams, playing Holiday's estranged husband, had a change of heart: "Early on in the shooting they come to the bathroom scene and Diana Ross throws a fit and Billy Dee has to fight for his life. I don't know, says Billy Dee, I don't know if she can *play* Billie Holiday—she *is* Billie Holiday. And Williams has got the scars to prove it."

Following her success in Lady Sings the Blues, *Ross received* Cue *magazine's Entertainer of the Year Award in January 1973. Here she proudly displays her plaque during the awards ceremony at New York's Tavern on the Green.*

Sidney Furie remembered Ross as a true professional on the set, calling her "as much of a pro as I have ever worked with in over 20 years of filmmaking." Producer Jay Weston agreed, calling Ross "the most incredible actress I've ever worked with." When *Lady Sings the Blues* was finally released near the end of 1972, one critic declared that "most of the credit [for the film's success] has to go to the little girl from the Supremes who comes up with the most extravagant and compassionate virtuoso star turn of the year." *Life* magazine declared, "Billie Holiday personified the vulnerability, terror, and confusion of the performer who can't hide in a crowd or in a role. Miss Ross, in an unself-conscious, bravura performance, makes us feel all of that." *Cue*, a film trade magazine, added, "If there's any justice, Diana Ross should be the biggest movie superstar to come along since Barbra Streisand, and she possesses deeper acting ability."

Even those who had been close to Billie Holiday were stunned by Ross's performance. One former friend of Holiday's, the jazz historian Leonard Feather, stated, "To my amazement . . . this newcomer destroyed all of my reservations. Miss Ross brought to her portrayal a sense of total immersion in her character. Dramatically, this is a tour de force." The following year, Ross was nominated for an Academy Award as Best Actress for her outstanding performance in the film. Although the Oscar ultimately went to Liza Minnelli, Ross took home *Cue* magazine's Entertainer of the Year Award along with a Golden Globe Award.

In 1970, Ross had married Bob Silberstein, a young Los Angeles publicist who had done some work with Motown. Although the marriage took many of her friends and family members by surprise, Ross proclaimed that she was deeply in love with Silberstein. The following year, on August 14, 1971, the

In this photo, Ross is flanked by her parents and her first husband, Bob Silberstein, whom she married in 1970.

couple's first child was born. The baby girl was named Rhonda Suzanne, and Ross found time to play the roles of both mother and wife in between her busy schedule of performing and filming *Lady Sings the Blues*. On October 29, 1972, just a few days after her film debuted in New York, Ross gave birth to her second child, Tracee Joy.

Soon after Tracee Joy was born, Ross was back on her feet with a number of television appearances, including two stints on "The Tonight Show," and spots on the "Today" show, "The Mike Douglas Show," "The Dick Cavett Show," "Jack Paar To-night," and a spot as the halftime entertainer at the Rose Bowl. Although she was constantly on the move, Ross always found a way to spend time with her growing family.

After the excitement of *Lady Sings the Blues* had died down a bit, Ross went back into the recording studio to work on a new song, "Touch Me in the Morning." The dreamy love song, released in May 1973, went on to reach number one on the pop charts, remaining on the charts for almost six months. Eventually, it was nominated for a Grammy Award. During the following year, Ross would also collaborate on three singles and an album with Marvin Gaye. One of the singles, "My Mistake Was To Love You," reached the top 20 on the pop charts and the top 10 on the rhythm and blues charts.

Meanwhile, in Europe, *Lady Sings the Blues* was giving Ross renewed credibility as a performer, and she was invited to France in 1973 to attend the prestigious Cannes Film Festival, where her film would be the most prominent entry. At Cannes, Ross performed a concert in front of an enthusiastic audience that included many of the most powerful players in show business. Following her show, the famed entertainer Josephine Baker, a black American expatriate who had been a major star in France since the 1920s, sought out Ross and congratulated her on her achievements as a singer and actress.

In the next two years, Ross would be immersed in what was perhaps her most ambitious project yet, the preparation and filming of her next movie, *Mahogany*. In this film, she starred as Tracy Chambers, an undervalued secretary living in the slums of Chicago and taking night school classes in fashion design. Chambers gets discovered by a prominent fashion photographer (Anthony Perkins of *Psycho* fame) and goes on to become a world-renowned fashion model and designer. In the dramatic finale of the movie, Tracy realizes that all of the money and fame in the world cannot buy love and happiness, and she returns

In a scene from Mahogany, Ross poses against the backdrop of a Roman fountain as Anthony Perkins prepares to photograph her. In addition to starring in the 1975 film, Ross also designed the costumes for the entire cast.

to Chicago to be with her true love, a political activist played by Billy Dee Williams.

In addition to her starring role, Ross provided music for the soundtrack and supervised the costume design for the entire cast. In a sense, *Mahogany* was the culmination of all Ross had dreamed of as a child. She acted and sang, two of her proven talents, but now she also put her longtime hobby of clothing design to use in true Hollywood style. "Designing the costumes," Ross said, "was a dream come true."

Mahogany was an ambitious (and costly) project on many counts. The filming took place in Chicago's depressed South Side, then in Rome, Italy, and finally in Los Angeles. It involved a much larger cast and film crew than *Lady Sings the Blues* and took much longer to complete.

As always, Ross threw herself into the hectic schedule with great determination. She spent weeks filming in one of Chicago's most dangerous neighborhoods, seeing firsthand the drugs and gang violence that had taken over the inner city by the mid-1970s.

After Chicago, she was off to the cosmopolitan glamour of Rome and the glitter of Los Angeles. Somewhere in the middle of her travels she found time to record the chart-busting song "The Theme from *Mahogany* (Do You Know Where You're Going To?)," a dramatic, fully orchestrated number that fades in and out during pivotal scenes of the film.

When *Mahogany* opened, it was an immediate box office success, easily covering the lavish cost of the transcontinental filming. The movie raked in $7 million in the first two weeks, and one popular movie theater in Manhattan held screenings around the clock to accommodate the massive crowds. Although a number of critics panned the film, the appreciation of moviegoers proved that Ross's performance had touched them deeply. And Ross's costume designs drew widespread praise, even from commentators who disliked the film.

As *Mahogany* stormed the theaters of America, Ross gave birth to her third child. On November 4, 1975, Chudney Lane Silberstein was born—like Diana, the name was another birth certificate mistake that stuck. Ross had intended to name her daughter Chutney after the sweet fruit relish, but the official certificate read Chudney.

As Ross's family was growing, another one close to her was sadly disintegrating. In February of 1976, Ross received the heartbreaking news that former Supreme Florence Ballard had died of a heart attack. Ballard had not fared well since leaving the trio in 1967, and Ross learned that Ballard's three young daughters faced a bleak financial future. In the spirit of family that had guided her all her life, Ross set up three extremely generous trust funds that the girls would be able to draw on when they turned 21. She attended Ballard's funeral in Detroit, asking for a moment of silence from the gathered crowd for her friend and fellow performer.

Despite such distressing events, success continued to follow Ross's efforts. Her latest single, "Love Hangover," which fit in with the new disco sound that was sweeping America, planted itself solidly at number one on three charts simultaneously—pop, rhythm and blues, and dance. Ross had also begun to work on an entirely new stage show for upcoming concerts. With a spectacular series of costume changes, as well as flashy dancers and musicians, "An Evening with Diana Ross" hit the stage at New York's Palace Theater in June 1976. The ticket sales broke a 63-year-old box office record for the theater, and the show later received a special Tony Award. Music critic Liz Smith wrote that Ross's show was "the warmest and best live performance I've ever seen."

The public's musical tastes were constantly shifting, and performers invariably fell by the wayside as new styles became popular. However, Ross showed again and again that she could roll with the punches. In the late 1970s she became a diva to disco fans around the world. An album of her greatest hits, which showcased all her different styles over the

During a record-breaking 1976 engagement at New York's Palace Theater, Ross cuddles with her children: (left to right) Rhonda Suzanne, Chudney Lane, and Tracee Joy. Later in the year, Ross decided to divorce her husband, end her long relationship with Motown, and begin a new life with her daughters in New York.

years, was popular with both longtime fans and the younger generation.

While she was maintaining her immense popularity with the public, Ross's personal life was becoming less satisfactory. She and her husband, Bob Silberstein, were having difficulties, and she was beginning to resent Berry Gordy's continued attempts to assert control over her career. During the filming of *Mahogany*, for instance, Gordy (who was the producer) had fired Academy Award–winning director Tony Richardson and decided to direct the film himself. To complicate the situation even further, Gordy and Silberstein often came into conflict as each tried to be the dominant force in Ross's life. "I tried to keep myself balanced in the desperate tug-of-war between the two of them with me in the center," Ross later recalled. "I couldn't. I felt torn apart all the time, not happy with Bob, not happy with Berry, not happy at Motown."

Ross finally decided that it was time to make a decisive break from the forces that seemed to be holding her back. In the summer of 1976, she initiated divorce proceedings against Silberstein and began to look for a way to end her relationship with Motown. Her next step was to move to New York with her three young daughters. Although she would always remain close to Gordy and continue to undertake film and music productions with Motown, Ross realized that she needed once again to carve out her own path. Thus as the 1970s drew to a close, a new company began to take shape—Diana Ross Enterprises, Inc., with Ross, not Gordy, at the helm. Living in New York with her own company in the works, Diana Ross was truly in command.

8

ONE STEP AT A TIME

IN SEPTEMBER 1977, filming commenced for a $30 million spectacular entitled *The Wiz*, a contemporary parable based on the classic 1939 film *The Wizard of Oz*. *The Wiz* had already been a critical and popular success as a Broadway musical, with its all-black cast and playful spin on the original 1939 movie.

The film starred Diana Ross as Dorothy, the role played in the 1939 version by Judy Garland. In the new version, Dorothy was not a Kansas farmgirl but a young schoolteacher in Harlem who winds up in the land of Oz after a blizzard. Michael Jackson costarred as the Scarecrow, and during the filming he and Ross solidified their friendship. The film also included performances by Richard Pryor as the Wiz and Lena Horne as the Good Witch. Renowned trumpeter and composer Quincy Jones (who would later collaborate with Michael Jackson on *Thriller*, which sold more copies than any previous record album) wrote the score for the movie musical. *The Wiz* was shot with the funky urban landscape of Manhattan as a backdrop.

The filming process was not without complications. Ross complained about the grueling choreography, which involved a great deal of running, and lamented the damage it did to her knees. Worse still was a frightening incident that followed the filming

A delighted Ross acknowledges the cheers of fans at a 1982 ceremony enshrining her in the Hollywood Walk of Fame. At this stage of her career, the multitalented Ross had become a legend on the entertainment scene.

of a scene where Dorothy is supposed to be meeting the Wiz for the first time. During that scene, Ross had to stare directly into a very bright light through a number of takes. After the day's shooting was finished, she noticed that she was having trouble seeing. Ross went immediately to an eye doctor, who told her that she had burned the retinas in both eyes. She was then flown to a world-renowned eye clinic in Maryland, where she spent several frightening days with her eyes bandaged, having been told by doctors that she might never fully regain her sight. Luckily, Ross recovered quickly and suffered little permanent damage—although she still must avoid bright lights and camera flashes.

The Wiz was finally released in the fall of 1978. Although the film was not a critical or box office success, Ross had few regrets about making it. She identified deeply with the role of Dorothy, and she welcomed the chance to sing on the silver screen. As she later revealed, "The film proved to be tremendously therapeutic for me, a strong vehicle in which to find myself."

Reflecting on *The Wiz*, Ross recalled the inner turmoil she was experiencing at the time, stemming from the ruptures that were taking place in her personal life. The songs, she said, "so perfectly related to what was going on inside of me: my fear of showing my true feelings, the confusion of being in a new and unfamiliar place, the isolation of being alone, having no friends, trying to find my way one step at a time." Not surprisingly, the music from *The Wiz* remains an important part of Ross's repertoire, and songs such as "Home" are staples of her concerts.

During her time of personal turmoil, Ross dated the actor Ryan O'Neal (with whom she was considering making a film) and, somewhat surprisingly, the glam-rock singer and bassist Gene Simmons of the band Kiss, whom she remained with for several years despite his habit of pursuing other women.

In 1980, after several years of soul-searching, Ross made her final break with Motown Records, the company that had given the Supremes their boost into the limelight and had guided Ross herself through 10 years of a solo career. "I did not leave Motown because I was upset or angry or hurt," she later insisted. "I left because I was growing as a person and it was time for me to move on." Motown had, in a sense, taken control over Ross's life. "All of these people were making decisions for me," she explained, "and I had no voice."

The songs Ross recorded immediately before leaving Motown provided a hint of her growing desire for artistic and personal freedom: "I'm Coming Out," penned by Nile Rodgers and Bernard Edwards, and "It's My Turn," by Michael Masser, the title song from a movie starring Michael Douglas. Another record

Ross's magic as a performer is conveyed in this scene from The Wiz, *in which she performs with Nipsey Russell (left) and Michael Jackson. Though bruised and nearly blinded by the ordeal of filming the 1978 musical, Ross derived a great deal of emotional fulfillment from the role of Dorothy.*

released at this time, "Upside Down," went to number one on the pop charts. The other two songs hit the top 10, and the album *Diana,* on which several of these songs appeared, went platinum and became one of the top-selling albums of Ross's career. After this flurry of success, it must have been quite a blow to Gordy and Motown when Ross announced that she would be striking out on her own.

After leaving Motown, Ross was snatched up by RCA Records, where she was given free rein to oversee all aspects of the production of her records— from selecting musicians to mixing and mastering to choosing the cover art. Her very first RCA album, *Why Do Fools Fall in Love?* included a title song that went to number one; the album, produced by Ross herself, went platinum.

Ross's fortunes during the 1980s proved that she had made a wise decision leaving Motown. Her records continued to be big sellers, including a number of collaborative efforts with some of the top performers of the day. Ross sang a duet on "Endless Love" with Lionel Richie, who was just beginning to branch out on a solo career after years with the Commodores. This theme song from the film of the same name went to number one in June 1981. It was also nominated for several Grammy Awards and earned an Academy Award nomination for Best Song in a Motion Picture. Richie and Ross performed the song live in March 1982 at the Academy Awards ceremony.

In 1982, Ross released a single entitled "Muscles," which had been written by Michael Jackson and was included on Ross's album *Silk Electric.* "Muscles" hit the top 10 on both pop and rhythm and blues charts and earned Ross another Grammy nomination; *Silk Electric* went gold.

The following year, Ross reunited with her old Motown friends to participate in a television special

entitled "Motown 25—Yesterday, Today, and Forever." The event brought together an array of early Motown luminaries with more recent stars, touching a chord in the hearts of the audience and the millions who watched at home. The Supremes, the Jackson Five, and the Miracles did magnificent reunion sets, and other performers included Stevie Wonder, Mary Wells, Marvin Gaye, the Temptations, and the Four Tops. Some of the gathered superstars, such as Ross and Michael Jackson, had moved on to other record labels, but one and all came back to pay tribute to the label that had given them their first big break. The show was a critical and popular success as well as a great emotional experience. It aired on NBC in May 1983, and proved to be the highest-rated musical special in television history. Later in the year, the show received an Emmy Award.

In 1984, Ross recorded "All of You" with her close friend Julio Iglesias and "Missing You," a Lionel Richie song. By the end of the year, "Missing You" reached number one on the rhythm and blues charts and reached the top 10 on the pop charts. Ross

With Diana Ross on hand to congratulate them, Eddie Holland (center), his brother Brian (second from right), and Lamont Dozier (left) are inducted into the Rock and Roll Hall of Fame in January 1990. Ross's brilliant legacy will always be linked to the classic Motown tunes composed by the Holland-Dozier-Holland songwriting team.

dedicated the song to Marvin Gaye, who had recently been murdered by his estranged father.

Ross's live performances continued to draw massive crowds. In 1982, she did a sold-out show at Giants Stadium in the New Jersey Meadowlands, accompanied by jazz legend Miles Davis. Her two benefit performances in New York's Central Park in 1983 drew close to a million fans and kicked off an extensive 45-city concert tour. Ross's 11 shows at Radio City Music Hall the following year broke box office records, taking in $1.7 million.

Ross was truly managing her own career at this point, but as she points out in her autobiography, her family always came first on her list of priorities. She spent more time than ever before with her three growing daughters, and her relationship with her mother was closer than ever. Sadly, Ernestine Ross died in October 1984, following a long, arduous battle with cancer. Friends remember that Ross was profoundly upset by the loss—in addition to the support her mother had given her throughout her career, she had also been a warm, loving companion to her granddaughters. During the difficult months following her mother's death, Ross found consolation among friends, particularly Julio Iglesias, with whom she and her children spent the Christmas holidays that year.

The following year, while vacationing with her daughters in the Bahamas, Ross met Arne Naess, a Norwegian shipping magnate who was vacationing with his own children after returning from a four-month-long journey to the summit of Mount Everest. Ross and Naess were married in a small town near Lausanne, Switzerland, less than a year later, in February 1986. The lavish wedding was attended by over 200 guests, and included performances by the remarkable Norwegian Boys Choir and Ross's long-time friend Stevie Wonder. After the wedding, Ross and Naess established their main residence in Connecticut and soon added two more children to their family. Ross Arne Naess was born on October 7, 1987, followed by another baby boy, Evan Olav, on August 26 of the following year.

Remarrying and becoming the mother of two more young children did not deter Ross from performing, recording, or engaging in the many activities of a world-famous superstar. She continued releasing her own solo material, including such albums as *Eaten Alive* (1985) and *Dirty Looks* (1987). In 1989, Ross re-signed with Motown Records, and released *Workin' Overtime* (1989) and *The Force Behind the Power* (1991), for which she embarked on a 15-month world tour. She also collaborated with Al B. Sure on the song "No Matter What You Do" in 1990. In 1992, she performed a set of jazz and blues numbers at the Ritz in New York, a performance that aired live on pay-per-view cable television.

In 1993, Ross published her heartfelt autobiography, *Secrets of a Sparrow*. Free of the incessant name dropping so endemic to celebrity autobiographies, *Secrets of a Sparrow* is less a chronicle of events than a vivid, emotional recollection of the most memorable scenes from Ross's exciting life. Along with an audiotape version narrated by Ross, the book gave readers a new look at the fiery and spirited woman behind the superstar.

Publishers Weekly raved about the audiotape version of *Secrets of a Sparrow*, reporting in November 1993 that "Ross's elegant, self-possessed voice casts a spell over the singer's reading of her autobiography. For Ross, memoir is a chance to spin a fairy-tale fable of struggle and redemption." According to Ross, writing the book was a form of therapy, helping her to discover herself as she wrote and giving her a chance to reflect on a career that had often seemed to pass in a blur of constant activity.

In February 1986, Ross married Norwegian shipping magnate Arne Naess. Though the wedding took place in a small town in Switzerland, it was a lavish affair, with 200 guests in attendance.

*Her stardom and glamour
undiminished, Ross celebrates
backstage with her three oldest
children—(left to right) Rhonda,
Tracee, and Chudney—after
opening an engagement at Radio
City Music Hall in 1991.*

In an interview for the *New York Times*, Ross said, "The early days of my career happened so fast that I didn't stop to think of the reason I did things. But I'm absolutely clear that I didn't do it for money. I did it for the love of the work, the singing. I'm still not clear about everything, but as I wrote the book I got a little more understanding of myself."

Around the same time as the book's release, Motown issued *Forever, Diana*, a retrospective set on four compact discs chronicling more than 30 years of Ross's work with the Supremes and as a solo performer. Meanwhile, Ross starred in a made-forteleision movie, "Out of Darkness," in which she played Paulie Cooper, a paranoid schizophrenic who had lost almost 20 years of her life to the debilitating mental illness before recovering with the aid of a new drug and the support of family and friends. The movie aired in January 1994 to enthusiastic reviews, marking another milestone in Ross's acting career.

Despite her many successes, not all of Ross's dreams have come to fruition. For many years, she has been attempting to find backing for a film about the life of Josephine Baker, in which she would play the title role, but she has been discouraged by Hollywood executives who believe that the film would not have enough commercial appeal. Naturally, some of her musical and dramatic efforts have met with less acclaim than others. Such are the highs and lows of a career spanning more than 30 years. "Dreams," Ross has said, "might not come when you want them. They come in their own time."

Throughout her career, Ross has served as an inspiration to a host of people in all walks of life: to aspiring actors and actresses; to singers, dancers, and fashion designers; to women and African Americans in general. "Singing—performing—is a gift," Ross has stated. "A divine gift. To be able to touch people all over the world with a record or a concert is truly a miracle." Perhaps the popular performer RuPaul summed up Ross's dynamic appeal best when he said, "First and foremost, first and always, my idol was and is Miss Diana Ross. She's someone who came up against adversity and just said, 'Uh-uh.'"

APPENDIX: SELECTED DISCOGRAPHY

◆◆◆

With the Supremes (Albums)

1963   Meet the Supremes
        A Bit of Liverpool

1964   Where Did Our Love Go?

1965   More Hits by the Supremes
        The Supremes at the Copa

1966   I Hear a Symphony
        The Supremes A-Go-Go

1967   The Supremes from Broadway to Hollywood
        The Supremes Sing Rodgers and Hart
        Diana Ross and the Supremes Greatest Hits, Volumes 1 and 2

1968   Reflections

1969   Love Child
        Diana Ross and the Supremes Greatest Hits, Volume 3

1970   Farewell

As Solo Performer (Albums)

1970   Diana Ross
        Everything Is Everything

1971   Diana! (original TV special sound track)
        Surrender
        Lady Sings the Blues (original motion picture sound track)

1973   Touch Me in the Morning
        Last Time I Saw Him

1974   Live! At Caesar's Palace

1975   Mahogany (original motion picture sound track)

1976   Diana Ross

1977   An Evening with Diana Ross
        Baby It's Me

1978	*Ross*
	Diana Ross Sings Songs from The Wiz
1979	*The Boss*
1980	*Diana*
1981	*To Love Again*
	Diana's Duets
	Why Do Fools Fall in Love?
1982	*Silk Electric*
1983	*Ross*
1984	*Swept Away*
1985	*Eaten Alive*
1987	*Red Hot Rhythm and Blues*
	Dirty Looks
1989	*Workin' Overtime*
1991	*The Force Behind the Power*
1993	*Forever, Diana*
1994	*One Woman*
1997	*Voice of Love*
1999	*Every Day Is A New Day*
2000	*Best of Diana Ross—Millennium*

CHRONOLOGY

———— ❧ ————

1944 Born Diana Ross in Detroit, Michigan, on March 26

1958 Enters Cass Technical High School and joins neighborhood singing group, the Primettes

1961 Primettes sign contract with Tamla Records and change name to the Supremes

1962 Ross graduates from Cass Tech; Supremes tour the country with Motor Town Revue

1964 Supremes release three number one singles; embark on tour of Europe; command nationwide audience with appearance on *The Ed Sullivan Show*

1965 Supremes embark on second European tour and headline at New York's Copacabana

1966 Supremes tour the Far East

1970 Ross makes final appearance as member of the Supremes; embarks on solo career and moves to California; marries Bob Silberstein

1971 Appears in her own television special "Diana!"; daughter Rhonda Suzanne is born

1972 Ross stars as Billie Holiday in *Lady Sings the Blues*; daughter Tracee Joy is born

1973 Ross wins *Cue* magazine's Entertainer of the Year Award

1975 Stars in film *Mahogany*; daughter Chudney Lane is born

1976 Ross decides to end her marriage; moves back to New York and starts her own production company

1978 Stars in film version of *The Wiz*

1980 Ends her long association with Motown and signs with RCA Records

1983 Gives two free concerts in New York's Central Park to raise money for a playground

1986 Marries Arne Naess

1987 Son Ross Arne is born

1988 Son Evan Olav is born

1989 Ross re-signs with Motown and embarks on 15-month world tour

1993 Autobiography, *Secrets of a Sparrow*, is published

1994 Ross stars in made-for-television movie "Out of Darkness"

1997 Releases *Voice of Love*, the 30th solo album of her career

1999 Hosts television miniseries "Motown 40: The Music Is Forever"; stars in television movie *Double Platinum*

2000 *Best of Diana Ross—Millennium* is released; reorganizes Supremes for Return to Love Tour, which is canceled after several dates

FURTHER READING

Benjaminson, Peter. *The Story of Motown.* New York: Grove Press, 1979.

Betrock, Alan. *Girl Groups: The Story of a Sound.* New York: Delilah, 1982.

George, Nelson. *The Death of Rhythm and Blues.* New York: Pantheon, 1988.

———. *Where Did Our Love Go?* New York: St. Martin's, 1985.

Gordy, Berry. *To Be Loved.* New York: Warner, 1995.

Kincaid, Jamaica. "Last of the Black White Girls." *Village Voice*, June 28, 1976.

Ross, Diana. *Secrets of a Sparrow.* New York: Villard, 1993.

Taraborrelli, Randy. *Call Her Miss Ross.* New York: Ballantine, 1989.

———. *Diana.* New York: Doubleday, 1985.

———. *Motown: Hot Wax, City Cool & Solid Gold.* New York: Doubleday, 1986.

Waller, Don. *The Motown Story.* New York: Scribner, 1985.

Wilson, Mary. *Dreamgirl: My Life as a Supreme.* New York: St. Martin's, 1986.

INDEX

PICTURE CREDITS

JOHN WYETH, JR., is a freelance writer living in New York and is an avid soul music and disco fan.

NATHAN IRVIN HUGGINS, one of America's leading scholars in the field of black studies, helped select the titles for the BLACK AMERICANS OF ACHIEVEMENT series, for which he also served as senior consulting editor. He was the W.E.B. Du Bois Professor of History and of Afro-American Studies at Harvard University and the director of the W.E.B. Du Bois Institute for Afro-American Research at Harvard. He received his doctorate from Harvard in 1962 and returned there as a professor in 1980 after teaching at Columbia University, the University of Massachusetts, Lake Forest College, and the California State University, Long Beach. He was the author of four books and dozens of articles, including *Black Odyssey: The Afro-American Ordeal in Slavery*, *The Harlem Renaissance*, and *Slave and Citizen: The Life of Frederick Douglass*, and was associated with the Children's Television Workshop, National Public Radio, the Boston Athenaeum, the Museum of Afro-American History, the Howard Thurman Educational Trust, and Upward Bound. Professor Huggins died in 1989, at the age of 62, in Cambridge, Massachusetts.